EVERYDAY MINISTRY

Tommy Kiker

SEMINARY HILL
PRESS

Table of Contents

Introduction

Every believer is called to the ministry of following Christ, serving the church, and sharing the Gospel. However, this book contends that there is a specific call to Christian leadership and focuses on that call, particularly the call to preach and pastoral ministry.

The material that follows certainly can be edifying to every church member, but it is geared toward the one who has surrendered vocationally to a call to pastoral ministry and is looking for encouragement in the midst of what is literally everyday ministry. The task is one that carries a heavy burden, overwhelming responsibility, and many other trials and tribulations. Jowett exclaims, "It is a great, awful, holy trust. We are called to be guides and guardians of the souls of men, leading them into 'the way of peace.'"[1]

To realize that you are called to a humanly impossible task with astounding pressures, countless assignments, and unreasonable expectations can, at times, be overwhelming. Paige Patterson exhorts that "life is hard, and ministry is harder."[2] There is an almost unending list of things for which the pastor is responsible. There is devotional time, Bible study, and sermon prep that is never-ending. The pastor should be a man of personal prayer, prayer for the body, prayer for the sick, and prayer for the lost. He should visit the lost, visit the sick, visit the church members. There is a fairly consistent demand for crisis counseling, marriage counseling, and financial counseling. The pastor is unable to avoid the constant phone calls,

---

[1]J.H. Jowett, *The Preacher His Life and Work* (New York: Harper & Brothers, 1912), 24.
[2]Paige Patterson, *A Field Guide for a Dangerous Call* (Fort Worth, TX: Seminary Hill Press, 2014), 43.

emails, drop-in visits, and SO MANY meetings. There are the demands of budgeting, staff meetings, vision casting, and other administrative tasks.

The ministry is a calling with endless needs and many never-finished tasks. The expectations are great, and the level of scrutiny is nearly unparalleled. You are on call 24/7, and without the supernatural strength of the Holy Spirit of God, you would surely fail.

The good news is that the Holy Spirit does intercede. It is vital that the minister has an intimate walk with Jesus, has been invited into the task of ministry, and labors with great focus. It is a terrible job, it is a difficult calling, but there is no other calling that brings such joy, excitement, and opportunities to see lives changed for the present and an eternity to come. The goal of this book is to provide a reminder of what God has called you to do, an encouragement toward that task, and hopefully a good number of tips along the way.

James Bryant and Mac Brunson describe pastoral ministry: "Being a pastor is perhaps the highest and noblest calling a man can receive. From the outside it may be viewed as a great privilege, and it is. But from the inside it is a great responsibility that encompasses back-breaking, mind-bending, heart-rending work with serious accountability to God."[3]

There are three absolutes that one considering pastoral ministry must evaluate in his life as he seeks God. The first seems fairly obvious but must be acknowledged: The man who seeks to enter pastoral ministry must be a child of God. Second, he must be called of God, and third, he must rightly discern that call so that it is sealed in his heart, mind, and spirit. The next two chapters discuss these absolutes, and the remainder of the work concentrates on how the minister functions day to day out of these foundational qualities.

---

[3]James Bryant and Mac Brunson, *The New Guidebook for Pastors* (Nashville, TN: Broadman & Holman, 2007), 7.

Chapter 1

Walk with Jesus
(Confidence in your Salvation)

There should not be need to even explain this necessity. How can one who has not been born again hope to be a pastor? However, there are those who have sought or been encouraged, pushed, or compelled into a career in ministry who have not had a genuine salvation experience and thus have no possibility of a genuine call to ministry.

There are many things that a minister must make certain before entering the ministry, but it is paramount that he has confidence in the eternal work of Christ having been accomplished in his heart and life. Richard Baxter exhorts pastors, "See that the work of grace be thoroughly wrought in your souls."[4] Mac Brunson adds, "Pastoral ministry should be a deeply spiritual ministry, involving who you are and not just what you do."[5]

In everyday ministry, the minister must pull from a source that goes well beyond his personal gifts and talents to the power of the Holy Spirit. An unredeemed minister has no such resource and is quickly overcome by the immensity of the work.

---

[4]Richard Baxter, *The Reformed Pastor*, Revised and Abridged by William Brown (Glasgow: William Collins, 1829), 91.
[5]Bryant and Brunson, *Guidebook for Pastors*, 6.

Gilbert Tennent, a prominent figure in the First Great Awakening, recognized the prominence of unconverted clergy during his day. It led him to preach a needed but controversial sermon, "The Dangers of an Unconverted Ministry." Jason Allen laments, "Nothing in the entire world is more tragic—or more ruinous to a church—than an unconverted minister."[6]

Every minister should deal diligently with Paul's admonition to the church at Philippi when he charges, "So then, my beloved, just as you have always obeyed, not as in my presence only, but now much more in my absence, work out your salvation with fear and trembling; for it is God who is at work in you, both to will and to work for His good pleasure" (Philippians 2:12–13). We recognize that salvation is from the Lord, but the minister must have a confidence that this relationship has been firmly established and that there is no unconfessed sin interfering with the fellowship between the minister and the Lord Jesus. Peter encourages all believers when he writes, "Therefore, brethren, be all the more diligent to make certain about His calling and choosing you; for as long as you practice these things, you will never stumble" (2 Peter 1:10).

If we are to minister to the people of God, we must be able to share with them that which we have personally experienced in our relationship with Him. Tozer explains this when he writes, "The minister must experience what he would teach or he will find himself in the impossible position of trying to drive sheep. For this reason he should seek to cultivate his own heart before he attempts to preach to the hearts of others."[7]

Make sure of your salvation, but as a minister, your relationship has to go beyond simply being born again. You must have a healthy, mature relationship with Christ if you are to serve in a worthy capacity.

---

[6]Jason Allen, *Discerning Your Call To Ministry: How to Know for Sure and What to Do About It* (Chicago, IL: Moody, 2016), 43.
[7]A.W. Tozer, "Sheep are Led" *Tozer for the Christian Leader: A 365-Day Devotional,* compiled by Ron Eggert (Chicago, IL: Moody, 2015), March 14 entry.

Personal Walk with Jesus

We will talk much more about the qualifications of the office of pastor in subsequent chapters, but let me introduce what I believe is the overarching qualification of a pastor, and that is the testimony of being blameless and above reproach. Titus 1:6 reads, "If any man is above reproach…," and verse 7, "For the overseer must be above reproach as God's steward." The corresponding passage in 1 Timothy 3:1–2 says, "If any man aspires to the office of overseer, it is a fine work he desires to do. An overseer, then, must be above reproach…."

A minister is above reproach (also translated "blameless") only in as much as he walks faithfully with Jesus. The consistent, overwhelming testimony of the minister's life must be one of blamelessness lest he be found unworthy of his calling.

Be reminded: This is not a call to sinless living. However, there should be no charge accurately lobbied against a minister of the Gospel that would cause the testimony of the Gospel to be marred.

One might argue, and rightly so, that these qualifications are for the office of pastor and do not necessarily need to be present in the life of every minister of the Gospel. I would contend that though these qualifications are presented for the office of elder, they are qualities for which every believer should aspire, and particularly those who would desire to minister in any capacity for the glory of Jesus.

As ministers, we must recognize that our very lives are a stewardship to Christ. We must manage every detail in a way that is blameless. MacArthur explains, "It is God's demand that His steward live in such a holy manner that his preaching would never be in contradiction of his lifestyle, that the pastor's indiscretions never bring shame on the ministry, and the shepherd's hypocrisy not undermine the flock's confidence in the ministry of God."[8]

---

[8]John MacArthur and the Master's Seminary Faculty, *Pastoral Ministry: How to Shepherd Biblically* (Nashville, TN: Thomas Nelson, 2005), 68.

Baxter pleads with the minister as he writes:

> O, brethren, watch therefore over your own hearts; keep
> out lusts and passions and worldly inclinations; keep up
> the life of faith and love and zeal; be much at home and be
> much with God. If it be not your daily business to study
> your own hearts, and to subdue corruption, and to walk
> with God—if you make not this a work to which you
> constantly attend all will go wrong, and you will starve
> your hearers; or, if you have an affected fervency, you
> cannot expect a blessing to attend it from on high. Above
> all, be much in secret prayer and meditation.[9]

The only way a minister is able to be presented blameless and
to remain blameless before the body of Christ is to be born again
and walk daily filled with the Spirit. The minister must maintain
an intimate relationship with the Lord Jesus Christ. Spurgeon
declares, "True and genuine piety is necessary as the first indispensable requisite; whatever 'call' a man may pretend to have, if he
has not been called to holiness, he certainly has not been called to
the ministry."[10]

There are plenty of spiritual disciplines that could be addressed
and are worthy of attention. For the sake of conciseness, the following three are the focus of our discussion: Bible study, prayer, and
personal evangelism.

Daily in the Word

How do you study other than sermon preparation? We must
take time to read the Word, study the Word, and be changed by
the Word. There certainly is much to be gained through the diligent study for sermons and other teaching opportunities, but I

---

[9]Baxter, *Reformed Pastor*, 103.

[10]C.H. Spurgeon, *Lectures to My Students*, Reprint (Grand Rapids, MI: Zondervan,
1972), 9.

exhort you to spend time reading Scripture for the primary purpose of devotion.

I have come to a place where it is nearly impossible for me to read
Scripture without thinking about how I might preach that Scripture. But the presence of this preaching element does not negate
the devotional aspect of the study. Every moment spent in Scripture, whether in personal quiet time or in preparation for teaching/
preaching, should have a genuine devotional element to it.

We do, however, need to guard time to be alone with Jesus that
is in some way separate from our normal toil. Jowett declares,

> We must sternly and systematically make time for prayer,
> and for the devotional reading of the Word of God. We
> must appoint private seasons for deliberate and personal
> appropriation of the Divine Word, for self-examination
> in the presence of its warnings, for self-humbling in
> the presence of its judgments, for self-heartening in the
> presence of its promises, and for self-invigoration in the
> presence of its glorious hopes. In the midst of our fussy,
> restless activities, in all the multitudinous trifles which,
> like a cloud of dust threaten to choke our souls, the
> minister must fence off his quiet and secluded hours, and
> suffer no interference or obtrusion.[11]

Certainly, the minister should spend more time studying Scripture than most any other task, probably even sleep itself on many
occasions. Much more concerning time spent in study and the
process of preparing and delivering sermons will be covered in
chapter 5.

Diligent in Prayer

If the minister is to walk in blamelessness, he must be a student
of the Word and he must be a man diligent in prayer. The minister
must spend consistent and extended time in prayer. Ministers are

---

[11]Jowett, *The Preacher*, 61–62.

busy and, sometimes, would even claim to be too busy to pray, but the truth is they are really too busy NOT to pray.

John Bisagno exhorts the pastor, "It is important to pray. In fact, it's most important to pray. Above everything else, be a person of prayer." He continues, "Constant prayer is commanded and commended, but that doesn't let you off the hook in the matter of longevity of prayer. Every pastor should spend at least an hour a day, seven days a week, on his knees before God in prayer."[12] Spurgeon warns, "If your zeal grows dull, you will not pray well in the pulpit, you will pray worse in the family, and worst in the study alone. When your soul becomes lean, your hearers, without knowing how or why, will find that your prayers in public have little savour for them; they will feel your barrenness, perhaps, before you perceive it yourself."[13]

There is a great lesson in Acts 6:2-4. In this passage, we see the appointment of what many argue are the first deacons. These men are set apart for the purpose of waiting tables and serving the widows. The twelve declare it is not good for them to neglect their primary tasks with such duties. The study of the Word is quickly recognized as a primary task of the pastor, but the passage makes clear that prayer is vital as well. The twelve argue, "It is not desirable for us to neglect the word of God in order to serve tables. ... But we will devote ourselves *to prayer* and to the ministry of the word" (emphasis added).

Jesus practiced frequent, consistent, and extended times of prayer. The Gospels clearly display the pattern of prayer in the life of Jesus:

- He would get alone to pray: "But Jesus Himself would often slip away to the wilderness and pray" (Luke 5:16).
- He would rise early to pray: "In the early morning, while it was still dark, Jesus got up, left the house, and went away to a secluded place, and was praying there" (Mark 1:35).

---

[12]Bisagno, *Pastor's Handbook*, 100–101.
[13]Spurgeon, *Lectures to My Students*, 14.

- He spent much time in prayer: "It was at this time that He went off to the mountain to pray, and He spent the whole night in prayer to God" (Luke 6:12).
- He exhorted others to pray: "Now He was telling them a parable to show that at all times they ought to pray and not to lose heart" (Luke 18:1).

Jesus taught His disciples to pray: "It happened that while Jesus was praying in a certain place, after He had finished, one of His disciples said to Him, 'Lord, teach us to pray just as John also taught his disciples'" (Luke 11:1).

It is interesting to note that the disciples observed Jesus' pattern of prayer and desired for Him to teach them to pray. The emphasis of prayer in the life of Jesus is clear and should be desirable for every believer, particularly the minister.

The minister is challenged and encouraged by the prayer life of the early church, as well. The pivotal moments in the establishing and function of the church as seen in the book of Acts are saturated in concentrated, diligent, and united prayer.

- Birth of the church at Pentecost—The church was born in the midst of a continual, unified prayer meeting: "These all with one mind were continually devoting themselves to prayer, along with the women, and Mary the mother of Jesus, and with His brothers" (Acts 1:14).
- Vital aspect of the early church—"They were continually devoting themselves to the apostles' teaching and to fellowship, to the breaking of bread and to prayer" (Acts 2:42).
- The appointment of deacons—Confirmation was made through the power of prayer: "… and after praying, they laid their hands on them" (Acts 6:6). Take note that the need for the new office was so that the apostles could focus on the primary objectives of their ministry: "But we will devote ourselves to prayer and to the ministry of the word" (Acts 6:4).

- The commissioning of church planters/missionaries—As the church continued to grow and attempt to fulfill the Lord's mandate to make disciples of all nations, prayer was a catalyst to the process: "While they were ministering to the Lord and fasting, the Holy Spirit said, 'Set apart for me Barnabas and Saul for the work to which I have called them.' Then, when they had fasted and prayed and laid their hands on them, they sent them away" (Acts 13:2-3).

The Scripture is clear that all believers are to be people of prayer, and the minister desperately needs to saturate his life with the presence, peace, and power of prayer. The minister should begin every day in prayer, continue the day in prayer, and end the day in prayer. He should recognize every opportunity presented to make prayer a priority in his personal life, in his family, and in the life of the church. Let us be reminded of Spurgeon's exhortation, "If there be any man under heaven, who is compelled to carry out the precept—'Pray without ceasing,' surely it is the Christian minister."[14]

Illustration of the power of prayer. There is much to be learned about prayer from the example of others. Have you ever heard of the name Daniel Nash? His tombstone gives a brief description. First of all, it reads, "Pastor, 1816-1822."

Nash served as a pastor for six years before some members of his church called for his dismissal, saying that he was too old (he was 46 at the time). After this hurtful experience, Nash removed himself from public ministry but continued in a vital role.

A second descriptor on his tombstone reads, "Laborer with Finney mighty in prayer." Even at a seminary, few have ever heard of Daniel Nash, but many have heard of Charles Finney, a prominent evangelist from the Second Great Awakening.

How did Nash serve with Finney? Through prayer. Much prayer. Constant, consistent prayer.

---

[14]Spurgeon, *Lectures to My Students*, 42.

The practice was for Nash to go ahead of Finney, find two or three like-minded believers, and begin to pray for God's movement in the area. After what was sometimes weeks of preparation through prayer, Finney would arrive for the meeting. Oftentimes, Nash would not even attend the services but would stay in a season of prayer.

Finney was absolutely convinced that the power of concentrated prayer was the effectual element of his preaching, and this was evident in two clear ways. First, if there seemed to be little effectiveness in the services, Finney would pause the event and petition Nash for greater fervency in prayer. Second, when Nash died, Finney ceased his itinerant ministry in a matter of months.

What's the point?

First, may we be reminded that God is not in need of our creativity, our great talent, our eloquence, or any other human element. If there is anything of any value, it comes from Him anyway. The truth is that we are desperately and completely dependent upon Him if we are to see any change with any eternal value.

Second, may God convict us to be men and women of consistent, fervent, and expectant prayer.

Third, may we commit to pray for those we know who stand consistently to preach and teach the Word of God. May we ask God to move in a way that is far beyond the norm and the expected. May God burden our hearts to see the results of His heart and not our efforts.

Finally, in the ministry, it is not only vital that you are a person of prayer, but that you surround yourself with others who are men and women of prayer. We have no power outside of what God grants, and the means through which we petition that power is prayer. We must have consistent, fervent, quality, and abundant prayer lives!

E.M. Bounds insists,

What the Church needs today is not more machinery or better, not new organizations or more and novel methods, but men whom the Holy Ghost can use—men of prayer, men mighty in prayer. The Holy Ghost does not flow

through methods, but through men. He does not come
on machinery, but on men. He does not anoint plans, but
men—men of prayer.[15]

An everyday minister who walks with Jesus walks in the power
of prayer!

 Practical Tip: When someone asks you to pray about something, stop whatever you are doing and pray right then.[16]

Consistent in Evangelism

An important aspect in maintaining an intimate relationship
with Jesus that gives power and encouragement is the consistent
sharing of the Gospel. There is no place for a pastor who does not
have a burden for souls.

The absence of consistent evangelism bears consequences due to
disobedience and a lack of the joy that comes from sharing the
Gospel. Spurgeon exclaims, "Though I can understand the possibility of an earnest sower never reaping, I cannot understand the
possibility of an earnest sower being content not to reap."[17]

How astonishing the fact that many pastors are content not
even sowing. The pastor, as much or maybe more than anyone else,
needs to be intentional in personal evangelism for several reasons.
The following highlights several personal blessings in consistent
evangelistic efforts.

Benefit of obedience: Obedience to God is always a positive
action. To clarify, though, evangelism is more than just being a

---

[15]E.M. Bounds, *Power through Prayer* rev. ed. (Grand Rapids, MI: Zondervan, 1962),
12.

[16]For more on this idea, see Tommy Kiker, "'Yeah, I'll Pray For You Later' – How To
Avoid The Lie," *Theological Matters* (February 16, 2016), http://theologicalmatters.
com/2016/02/16/yeah-ill-pray-for-you-later-how-to-avoid-the-lie/.

[17]Charles Spurgeon, "Serving the Lord with Gladness," in *Metropolitan Tabernacle
Pulpit* (London: Passmore and Alabaster, 1868; reprint, Pasadena, TX: Pilgrim
Publications, 1989), vol. 13, 495–496.

good example. Many have declared, "Always share the Gospel, use words when necessary." That phrase has never made much sense to me. It is much like saying, "Go feed the starving, use food if necessary."

The Gospel contains words, and we have been commanded to share those words with a dying and desperate world. Jesus commanded us to go into all the earth and make disciples. Obedience to that command leads to consistent evangelism. There is more to be done after evangelism, but the rest cannot be done without evangelism.

The pastor must recognize that evangelism requires intentionality. The temptation arises to consider the preaching, counseling, and other pastoral duties as a substitute for intentional evangelism. While all our other activities should be saturated with evangelistic fervor, such activity does not relieve us of the responsibility of reaching our family, friends, and neighbors who never enter our building.

MacArthur reminds us, "Evangelism for the believer is not a gift, nor is it an option. It is a command; one he should be careful to obey!"[18] There are many commendable plans for personal evangelism. Every pastor in obedience needs to make sure he has an intentional plan.

Benefit of hearing the Gospel: A second benefit of intentionally sharing the Gospel is the reminder that it brings to the one sharing. Evangelism is Gospel preaching and must contain the content of the Gospel: Jesus came to earth, lived a perfect life, was crucified for the sin of all, and was resurrected on the third day. If you have not shared the death, burial, and resurrection of Jesus, you have not shared the Gospel. However, when sharing the Gospel, it never grows old to any believer who hears it. Even if the individual to whom you are witnessing rejects the Gospel, you have been reminded of the love of Christ through His death, burial, and glorious resurrection.

---

[18]MacArthur, *Pastoral Ministry*, 253.

Encouragement of unseen fruit: If the pastor is consistently sharing the Gospel in his preaching, teaching, and individual encounters, he can have a confidence that God is working through His Word. Isaiah 55:11 declares that the Word of God does not return void. I am convinced that the content of the Gospel unleashed can bring about fruit long after it is initially heard. Trust that if you are faithful to sow, God is faithful to bring the harvest. Certainly, there is great joy in reaping the harvest, but we should find great joy in planting the seeds, as well.

 Practical Tips for Evangelism. Saturate your evangelism efforts with prayer. Pray for your family, neighbors, and those you meet and get to know at your children's activities. As we go through our day-to-day activities, God brings many people into our paths. Many of these He intends to receive a Gospel witness from us.

There are many ways to be more intentional in your evangelism. One simple tip I have used for nearly two decades now is to take a moment when I go out to eat and ask my server if there is any way I can pray for him or her. I say something like this: "What's your name? Well, (name), we always like to ask the Lord to bless our food before we eat, and we always like to ask our server if there is any way we can pray for him or her...?"

Just a simple offer, but you are going to be amazed at the responses you receive. Very rarely, it may result in a little awkward moment, but the vast majority of people (about 95 percent of the time, in my experience) will, at the very least, be grateful for the gesture. There have been countless times that we were greatly thanked and given very specific prayer requests. Many times, we have been able to share some or all of the Gospel. There have even been several times we have had the joyous opportunity to lead someone to the Lord.[19]

---

[19]For more on being a personal soul winner, including how to create a culture of

Conclusion

The three main tasks that we have as pastors are embodied in the three previously mentioned disciplines. Pastors have a mandate to feed the sheep, but they are unable to do so if they are not being fed by consistent Bible intake themselves. Pastors also have a burden to pray for the flock and to teach them to pray, but one cannot teach well what he does not practice himself. Finally, pastors have an obligation to be fishers of men and to train others in this task.

Because of the great difficulty of the ministry—and the impossibility of such a task without the direct intervention of the Spirit of God—Jowett reminds the minister, "hold firmly and steadily to this primary principle, that of all things that need doing this need is supreme, to live in intimate fellowship with God."[20] A pastor succeeds in having an intimate relationship with Christ when he is in the Word, in prayer, and faithfully sharing the Gospel.

---

everyday evangelism within your church, see Matt Queen, *Everyday Evangelism* (Fort Worth, TX: Seminary Hill Press, 2015).

[20]Jowett, *The Preacher*, 63.

Chapter 2

Called by Jesus
(Confidence in your Call)

Nearly as dangerous as entering the ministry unredeemed is entering the ministry without a divine mandate. In using the terminology of a "call," I am speaking mainly concerning a call to ministry leadership, and even more specifically the call to pastoral ministry.

"It does not matter how you start if you do not finish!" Maybe you have heard this exhortation at a pastor's conference or some kind of training session for pastors. The statement implies that if one is to win a race, he must not only start strong, but he must actually finish the race.

Let us think about the phrase in a more complete light. True, it does not matter how you start if you do not finish, but it does matter how you start if you plan on finishing well.

Since 2008, the sprinting world has been amazed by the feats of sprinter Usain Bolt. He has been nearly unbeatable in the 100-meter and 200-meter sprints. On August 28, 2011, at the world championships held in South Korea, the only real question heading into the 100-meter event was whether Bolt would best his own world record time. The only problem was that Bolt jumped before the firing of the starter's pistol, and so before the race even began, he was disqualified.

One might also remember the name of sprinter Ben Johnson. He won the 1988 Olympic Gold medal in the 100-meter, only to have it stripped away because of his use of banned substances.

How we start matters; how we run matters; and not only that we finish, but how we finish matters. The purpose of the next couple of chapters is to help the reader gain an understanding of what it means to be called to the ministry, how to discern that call, and how to guard one's character in order to live out that call from beginning to end. There must be a firm foundation on which to build a lifetime of ministry. If not, a minister may finish poorly, or be disqualified before finishing at all.

Start Well, Run Well, Finish Well!

Not that I have already obtained it or have already become perfect, but I press on so that I may lay hold of that for which also I was laid hold of by Christ Jesus. Brethren, I do not regard myself as having laid hold of it yet; but one thing I do: forgetting what lies behind and reaching forward to what lies ahead, I press on toward the goal for the prize of the upward call of God in Christ Jesus (Philippians 3:12-14).

L.R. Scarborough argues, "A divine call is a spiritual necessity to a Gospel ministry. He who goes out without God's call has no promise of God's power. The task is too great for us unless our hearts are assured that God has sent us."[21]

Edwin Lutzer adds, "I don't see how anyone could survive ministry if he felt it was just his own choice. ... They [ministers] are sustained by the knowledge that God has placed them where they are. Ministers without such conviction often lack courage and carry their resignation letter in their coat pocket. At the slightest hint of difficulty, they're gone."[22] Leigh Richmond says, "The national church ... groans and bleeds from the crown of its

---

[21]L.R. Scarborough, *Recruits for World Conquests* (New York: Fleming H. Revell, 1914), 35.

[22]Edwin Lutzer, *Pastor to Pastor* (Grand Rapids, MI: Kregel, 2008), 11.

head to the sole of its feet from the daily intrusion of unworthy men into the Ministry."[23]

I like the very practical reminder given by long-time pastor and denominational leader Jimmy Draper. He writes, "The ministry is a terrible vocation … but a wonderful calling."[24]

Finally, Spurgeon, the "prince of preachers," writes, "In the present dispensation, the priesthood is common to all the saints; but to prophesy, or what is analogous thereto, namely, to be moved by the Holy Ghost to give oneself up wholly to the proclamation of the gospel, is, as a matter of fact, the gift and calling of only a comparatively small number; and surely these need to be as sure of the rightfulness of their position as were the prophets; and yet how can they justify their office, except by a similar call."[25]

There are those who would argue there is no such thing as a specific call to pastoral ministry. Some would argue that people can decide in their own wisdom that they should enter the ministry. Others would argue that all followers of Christ have a call to ministry (and rightly so), but in so doing negate the need for a specific call to pastoral ministry, thus overstating their argument. The Scripture gives many accounts as evidence for the necessity of a specific call to ministry assignments.

Foundational Evidence: Old Testament. The consistent theme in the Old Testament concerning the work of the priests and prophets is that they were appointed (called) by God. The Scripture proclaims that a prophet not called of God would be useless to the people: "'Behold, I am against those who have prophesied false dreams,' declares the Lord, 'and related them and led My people astray by their falsehoods and reckless boasting; yet I did not send them or command them, nor do they furnish this people the slightest benefit,' declares the Lord" (Jeremiah 23:32).

In Numbers 18, when God establishes the line of the priesthood, clearly any unauthorized person who even comes near the sanctuary

---

[23] *Life of Leigh Richmond*, 475, quoted in Bridges, 93.
[24] Jimmy Draper, *Don't Quit Before You Finish* (Franklin, TN: Clovercroft, 2015), 2.
[25] Spurgeon, *Lectures to My Students*, 25.

19

should be put to death (Numbers 18:7). Bridges writes, "Under the old dispensation, intrusion into the priestly office was marked as the most dangerous presumption."[26] Such a mistake would prove very costly to anyone who made it.[27]

The prophets never assumed a personal mandate to proclaim, "Thus says the Lord...," but rather responded, oftentimes reluctantly, to the personal call of God. Isaiah's call in Isaiah 6 is an example of such an encounter with God. For Isaiah, the only right response was surrender, and only then did God give him a specific assignment.

Jeremiah was rather reluctant when God called him to prophesy. Jeremiah protested over his age and ability to speak, but God had already appointed him a prophet and set him apart for a specific task.

Over and over again in the prophetic books, there is language that points to a personal call:

- "As He [God] spoke to me the Spirit entered me and set me on my feet; and I heard Him speaking to me. Then He said to me, 'Son of man, I am sending you to the sons of Israel...'" (Ezekiel 2-3).
- "Then Amos replied to Amaziah, 'I am not a prophet, nor am I the son of a prophet; for I am a herdsman and a grower of sycamore figs. But the Lord took me from following the flock and the Lord said to me, 'Go prophesy to My people Israel'" (Amos 7:14-15).
- "The word of the Lord came to Jonah the son of Amittai saying, 'Arise, go to Nineveh the great city and cry against it, for their wickedness has come up before Me'" (Jonah 1:1-2).

---

[26]Charles Bridges, *The Christian Ministry* (London: Seeley, Burnside, and Seeley, 1844), 90.
[27]See, for example, 2 Chronicles 26:16-21, wherein King Uzziah burns incense in the temple, contrary to God's law. The priests chastise him for doing so, but he continues anyway. As punishment for this unfaithfulness to the Lord, Uzziah immediately becomes leprous and is rushed out of the temple. He dies a leper, "cut off from the house of the Lord" (verse 21).

- "Now the word of the Lord came to Jonah the second time, saying, 'Arise, go to Nineveh the great city and proclaim to it the proclamation which I am going to tell you.' So Jonah arose and went to Nineveh according to the word of the Lord" (Jonah 3:1-3).

The call of Isaiah, Moses, and many others in the Old Testament contained a clearly supernatural element. I would argue that any God-given call today maintains a supernatural element, but that element is accomplished through the clear work of the Holy Spirit and has no need of a physical and/or outward manifestation of God's supernatural presence. Obviously, we should not make a direct correlation between the call of the priests and prophets to the call of ministers today, but Spurgeon is correct when he argues: "These need to be as sure of the rightfulness of their position as were the prophets; and yet how can they justify their office, except by a similar call."[28]

Foundational Evidence: New Testament. The examples are in no way limited to the Old Testament; the New Testament contains a plethora of call experiences, as well. The call of the apostles is covered several places in the Gospels. John 1:19ff describes the calling of Andrew and Peter, and then Philip and Nathanael. Matthew 4:18ff, Mark 1:16-20, and Luke 5:1-11 give accounts of the calling of Andrew, Peter, James, and John. Mark 2:13-17 shares the encounter and call that Matthew had with Jesus (also Matthew 9:9–13; Luke 5:27–32).

The selection of the entire twelve is described in Mark 3:13–19, Luke 6:12–16, and Matthew 10:1–4. Jesus called all to follow after Him, but there was a specific call on these twelve. In the same way, God calls all to follow after Him through Christ, but He calls specific individuals to specific tasks.

Other examples of calling in the New Testament include the call of Paul on the road to Damascus and later the setting apart of Paul and Barnabas by the church at Antioch. The significance of

[28]Spurgeon, *Lectures to My Students*, 25.

the Acts 13 passage is the affirmation of the authority and responsibility of the local church to affirm those set apart for the work of the Lord.

Acts 13:1–3 shows the pattern of the church following the leading of the Holy Spirit and setting aside men to the work of the ministry. The Bible says, "While they were ministering to the Lord and fasting, the Holy Spirit said, 'Set apart for me Barnabas and Saul for the work to which I have called them.' Then, when they had fasted and prayed and laid their hands on them, they sent them away."

The call came from God and was confirmed by the church. The significance of this pattern will be further discussed later regarding how one discerns a call to ministry.

The apostle Paul uses call language in the introduction of most of his letters. Bridges writes of Paul, "How plainly do the superscriptions of St. Paul's Epistles, with one or two exceptions, stamp his instructions to the churches with the seal of his heavenly commission! He is never weary of inculcating on us this truth—that the will of God is the sole rule of any man's call, and the only gate by which he can enter into the Ministry."[29]

The call language is emphatic in other parts of the New Testament, as well. In Paul's address to the elders at Ephesus, he says, "Be on guard for yourselves and for all the flock, among which *the Holy Spirit has made you overseers*, to shepherd the church of God which He purchased with His own blood" (Acts 20:28, emphasis added). Peter uses similar language when he writes, "Shepherd the flock of God among you, exercising oversight not under compulsion, but voluntarily, *according to the will of God*; and not for sordid gain, but with eagerness; nor yet as lording it over *those allotted to your charge*, but proving to be examples to the flock. And when the Chief Shepherd appears, you will receive the unfading crown of glory" (1 Peter 5:2-4, emphasis added).

Furthermore, one can discern a divine call for the preacher in Paul's teaching in Romans 10:14–15: "How then will they call on

---

[29]Bridges, *The Christian Ministry*, 92.

Him in whom they have not believed? How will they believe in Him whom they have not heard? And how will they hear without a preacher? How will they preach *unless they are sent?*" (emphasis added). Who else has authority to send the preacher to proclaim the Gospel other than God Himself?

After looking at the idea of a call to Christian leadership from a practical and a biblical perspective, may I suggest the following as a helpful definition of a call to ministry:

> *A directive received as one walks intimately with the Lord and is obedient to His leading. It will always be in agreement with and in no way contrary to the clear teaching of Scripture. A call is more than a "leaning" or a "feeling" but rather a conviction that would be sinful to disobey.*

I certainly do not suggest that the conversation is over and the definition of a call to ministry has been settled. However, if one is convinced that there is such a thing as a call to pastoral ministry or some other specific Christian ministry, the next logical question is how one can discern such a call.

Charles Bridges writes, "The two grand combining requisites for this 'Divine vocation' may be determined to be a desire and a fitness for the office."[30] The focus of this section claims the qualifications for pastoral ministry are the greatest tools in discerning the legitimacy of a call to pastoral ministry in our own lives and in the lives of others.

If someone thinks there is a call of God on his life to pastoral ministry, the qualifications given in 1 Timothy 3 and Titus 1 can certainly test the genuineness of that call. John MacArthur writes, "The call to the ministry is not a matter of analyzing one's talents and then selecting the best career option. It's a Spirit-generated compulsion to be a man of God and serve Him in the church. Those who God calls will meet the (biblical) qualifications."[31]

---

[30]Ibid., 94.
[31]John MacArthur, *The Master's Plan for the Church* (Chicago, IL: Moody, 2008), 244.

When discerning a personal call or even the call of someone else, we must not let feelings interfere with biblical truth. Gerald Cowen writes, "When there are things in one's history that disqualify one from serving, subjective feelings should not override the qualifications given in Scripture."[32] Terry Wilder, professor of New Testament at Southwestern Baptist Theological Seminary, argues, "If God has called you to be a pastor, or for that matter, to any place of Christian Service, your call to ministry cannot be considered separately from what God has revealed in His Word."[33]

Our call is most accurately discerned not by human emotion or circumstances, but by a clear examination of our fitness to the call based on the qualifications given to us in the authoritative Word of God. The very fact that the New Testament offers clear guidelines by which a man is qualified to hold the office of pastor gives evidence that it is not something to be entered into without invitation and much discernment by the individual and the church.

It is a trustworthy statement: if any man aspires to the office of overseer, it is a fine work he desires to do. An overseer, then, must be above reproach, the husband of one wife, temperate, prudent, respectable, hospitable, able to teach, not addicted to wine or pugnacious, but gentle, peaceable, free from the love of money. He must be one who manages his own household well, keeping his children under control with all dignity (but if a man does not know how to manage his own household, how will he take care of the church of God?), and not a new convert, so that he will not become conceited and fall into the condemnation incurred by the devil. And he must have a good reputation with those outside the church, so that he will not fall into reproach and the snare of the devil. (1 Timothy 3:1-7)

---

[32]Gerald P. Cowen, *Who Rules the Church* (Nashville, TN: Broadman & Holman), 30.
[33]Terry Wilder, *Answering the Call: Examining God's Call to Christian Service* (Kansas City, MO: Midwestern Baptist Theological Seminary, 2010), 4.

For this reason I left you in Crete, that you would set in order what remains and appoint elders in every city as I directed you, namely, if any man is above reproach, the husband of one wife, having children who believe, not accused of dissipation or rebellion. For the overseer must be above reproach as God's steward, not self-willed, not quick-tempered, not addicted to wine, not pugnacious, not fond of sordid gain, but hospitable, loving what is good, sensible, just, devout, self-controlled, holding fast the faithful word which is in accordance with the teaching, so that he will be able both to exhort in sound doctrine and to refute those who contradict. (Titus 1:5-9)

1 Timothy 3 and Titus 1 provide clear guidelines regarding what qualifications should *already* be evident in the life of the man who would hold the office of pastor. However, just because one might give evidence of meeting the qualifications does not automatically suggest that he should serve in the pastoral office. The qualifications are spiritual characteristics for which all believers should strive, and we would hope many, even most, would live a life that exemplifies these characteristics.

So how would one, after examining the qualifications, determine whether he is certainly qualified and called to pastoral ministry?

Would you agree that to make such a declaration would appear somewhat arrogant? So what should we suggest to those who are wrestling with a call to preach and a call to pastor?

I believe one of the classic answers is found in Spurgeon's *Lectures to My Students*, specifically in the second chapter, which is entitled, "The Call to the Ministry." Spurgeon gives at least five signs he believes are present in the life and circumstances of one genuinely called to ministry:

1. An intense, all-absorbing desire for the work. We have all heard, "If you can do anything else, then do it!" Spurgeon argues that if you could be content doing any other work, then you most certainly should do it. He exclaims, "A man so filled with God would utterly weary of any pursuit but that for which his inmost soul pants."[34]

Spurgeon clarifies that this desire must be one that is God-honoring, not self-promoting. He explains, "If a man can detect, after the most earnest self-examination, any other motive than the glory of God and the good of souls in his seeking the bishopric, he had better turn aside from it at once; for the Lord will abhor the bringing of buyers and sellers into his temple."[35]

A desire alone does not negate the qualifications, nor does it automatically confirm a calling. Bridges explains, "The two grand combining requisites for this 'Divine vocation' may be determined to be a desire and a fitness for the office." He continues, "So important, however, is the combination of desire, and capacity, that neither, separated from the other, can be deemed sufficient."[36]

2. Aptness to teach and some measure of the other qualities needful for the office of a public instructor. There should be some level of giftedness for the work. Certainly, the Lord can supernaturally fill the void, but normally, there should be a level of readiness for the duties required in the work of the office.

3. He must see a measure of conversion work going on under his efforts or he may conclude that he has made a mistake. Spurgeon argues that if a man is genuinely called to preach, he will see a measure of conversion work taking place in his preaching and ministry efforts. He writes, "I could never be satisfied with a full congregation, and the kind expression of friends; I longed to hear that hearts had been broken, that tears had been streaming from the eyes of the penitents. ... There must be some measure of conversion work in your irregular labors before you can believe that preaching is to be your lifework."

He continues by declaring that he cannot understand "how men continue at ease in preaching year after year without conversions." He concludes, "The meanest occupation confers some benefit upon

---

[34] Spurgeon, *Lectures to My Students*, 28.
[35] Ibid.
[36] Bridges, *The Christian Ministry*, 94, 99.

mankind, but the wretched man who occupies the pulpit and never glorifies his God by conversions is a blank, a blot, an eyesore, a mischief ... and meanwhile the transient barrenness will fill the soul with unutterable anguish. Brethren, if the Lord gives you no zeal for souls, keep to the lapstone or the trowel, but avoid the pulpit as you value your heart's peace and your future salvation."[37]

I would argue that the pastor who preaches year after year and sees no one come to Christ, and it does NOT burden his soul, is not worthy of the call of Christ Jesus!

4. The will of the Lord concerning pastors is made known through the prayerful judgment of his church. Spurgeon is right when he declares that the church is a powerful authority on the legitimacy and genuineness of one's calling. He writes, "Churches are not all wise, neither do they all judge in the power of the Holy Ghost, but many of them judge after the flesh; yet I had sooner accept the opinion of a company of the Lord's people than my own upon so personal a subject as my own gifts and graces."[38]

If an individual claims the call of God on his life but does not have the confirmation of a local body of believers, it should cause great hesitation on the part of those who might consider coming under his teaching.

5. If your call from the Lord be a real one, you will not long be silent. God will grant opportunity to those He has called to serve Him in preaching and in the office of the pastor. Spurgeon warns, "Do not run about inviting yourselves to preach here and there; be more concerned about your ability than your opportunity, and more earnest about your walk with God than about either."[39]

We must consider a word of warning in the area of opportunity so that we do not too narrowly define a genuine opportunity. If you are not willing to serve the Lord in proclaiming the Gospel in a less prominent venue, then you are not worthy to represent the Lord in any venue.

---

[37]Spurgeon, *Lectures to My Students*, 31-32.
[38]Ibid., 32–33.
[39]Ibid., 33.

There is value in Spurgeon's description of how one might know he IS called to the ministry, but he gives several ways someone might know he is NOT called, as well. He writes, "Young brethren apply who earnestly desire to enter the ministry, but it is painfully apparent that their main motive is an ambitious desire to shine among men."[40] Spurgeon explains, "They have embraced the idea that if they entered the ministry they would be greatly distinguished; they have felt the buddings of genius, and have regarded themselves as greater than ordinary persons, and, therefore, they have looked upon the ministry as a platform upon which to display their supposed abilities."[41] He concludes, "We find that we have nothing whereof to glory, and if we had, the very worst place in which to hang it out would be a pulpit; for there we are brought daily to feel our own insignificance and nothingness."[42]

Iorg agrees, saying, "If you want to be in ministry leadership, be sure your desire is in response to God's call and not to satisfy your unrealistic expectations about the ministry."[43] Spurgeon continues, "So, too, those who cannot endure hardness, but are of the kid-gloved order, I refer elsewhere."[44]

If you get your feelings hurt easily, you might want to avoid ministry altogether, and certainly any public ministry. If you have to be convinced that everyone likes you and is happy with the way you are doing things, ministry is not for you. You will find yourself in a miserable state.

Gain peace in knowing that you are being obedient to the Lord. It is not Christ-like to avoid considering what people think about you; you are called to serve them. However, it is also not Christ-like to find your security in anyone other than Christ Himself.

Another category of ministry candidates who should be dismissed are those who see ministry as a last resort. Spurgeon exclaims, "One brother I have encountered—one did I say? I have

[40]Ibid., 35-36.
[41]Ibid.
[42]Ibid.
[43]Iorg, *Is God Calling Me*, 68.
[44]Spurgeon, *Lectures to My Students*, 36.

met ten, twenty, a hundred brethren, who have pleaded that they were sure, quite sure that they were called to the ministry—they were quite certain of it, because they had failed in everything else."[45]

Here is one that may have been rectified since Spurgeon's day, but still interesting. Spurgeon writes, "That narrow chest does not indicate a man formed for public speech. You may think it odd, but still I feel very well assured, that when a man has a contracted chest, with no distance between his shoulders, the all-wise Creator did not intend him habitually to preach. If he had meant him to speak he would have given him in some measure breadth of chest, sufficient to yield a reasonable amount of lung force."[46]

I would add at least one more attitude that shows one is not genuinely called to pastor, and that is if he has what I call the "Mighty Mouse" syndrome. As you may remember from the old cartoon, when the superhero mouse would get ready to leap into action, he would yell, "Here I come to save the day!" There seem to be way too many preachers who think the church has lamented for hundreds of years, and now, finally, they are here to save the poor thing.

Let me assure all of us: Christ's church is not in need of a savior; she already has a spotless One! However, in God's sovereign plan, I do believe she could benefit from a flood of God-called, Spirit-filled, biblically qualified, passionately evangelistic, and theologically sound pastors!

Spurgeon concludes his lecture with this exhortation:

> We must try whether we can endure brow-beating, weariness, slander, jeering, and hardship; and whether we can be made the off-scouring of all things, and be treated as nothing for Christ's sake. If we can endure all these, we have some of those points which indicate the possession of the rare qualities which should meet in a true servant of the Lord Jesus Christ.[47]

---

[45]Ibid., 37.
[46]Ibid., 36–37.
[47]Ibid., 40.

Only those with a genuine call should or would volunteer for such a task.

Patterson warns the unsure,

> Do not mount this sled known as the "pastorate" unless you have a clear mandate from Heaven. It looks fun when watching others do it. But the experience of serving as pastor is fraught with treacherous curves, mountainous bumps, and immovable objects. If you have accepted the call because of the prestige of being "the [Preacher]" or for rewards that are admittedly enormous or because you have been favorably impressed with your own comprehension of theology and rhetorical skills or for any lesser reason than the sure call of God, then I can faithfully advise you that you will be one miserable human before the ride is over.[48]

Take great confidence in your call; there are going to be days when it is one of your greatest comforts. Jowett warns, "If we lose the sense of the wonder of our commission we shall become like common traders in a common market, babbling about common wares."[49] We endure the difficulties of ministry because of our confidence in our call and, more importantly, our confidence in the One who calls us!

 Practical Tip: Do you feel a leaning toward a call to ministry—a call to preach or to be a pastor? Talk with your pastor; share what God is doing in your life. Invite mature believers into the conversation, examine the qualification passages carefully, and prayerfully walk through the process.

I would suggest that you read through Spurgeon's chapter on the call. I also recommend the following four works on discerning the call by three Southern Baptist seminary presidents:

---

[48]Paige Patterson, *So You Have Been Called to a Church* (Wake Forest, NC: Magnolia Hill Papers, 1996), 3-4.
[49]Jowett, *The Preacher*, 21.

Jason Allen, *Discerning Your Call to Ministry* (Chicago, IL: Moody, 2016).

Jeff Iorg, *Is God Calling Me* (Nashville, TN: Broadman & Holman, 2008).

Paige Patterson, *A Field Guide for a Dangerous Call* (Fort Worth, TX: Seminary Hill Press, 2014).

Paige Patterson, Thomas White, and L.R. Scarborough, *Calling Out the Called* (Fort Worth, TX: Seminary Hill Press, 2008).

These four resources can help raise and answer many of the questions you need to consider when discerning a call to ministry.

One word of advice: If you quickly lose interest in the discussion, you might assume that you are not called, at least not at this particular time. The one called of God has GREAT difficulty losing interest in pursuing that invitation.

Make sure of your call; it remains a great source of encouragement and strength. I appreciate the way Allen conveys the necessity of a call and confidence in the call. He writes,

Even the best of ministries can be challenging enough, but to undertake ministry without a clear sense of God's call, accompanied by God's power and God's favor, is too much to bear. At the same time, God's call is too noble, too consequential, and too glorious to neglect. You need to know for sure whether God has called you. And you can.[50]

---

[50] Allen, *Discerning Your Call*, 16.

Chapter 3

Qualifications Lead to Function
(Confidence in Character)

A pastor's life must bear evidence of a consistent attainment of the qualifications granted in the New Testament for the office. These qualifications are not to be met at one particular instance, but in a continual testimony of "blamelessness." Allen agrees, "The qualifications do not represent a one-time threshold to cross. Rather, they mark a lifestyle to be maintained, character to be cultivated, and ongoing accountability to God's Word and God's people."[51]

The qualifications use such language as to make clear that one in the office of pastor must have a reputation of exemplary character in thought and deed. Words such as "temperate," "sober-minded," "of good behavior," "holy," and "self-controlled" make this obvious. They all point to one who walks in control of his actions through the power of the Holy Spirit. MacArthur exclaims, "If a man cannot control his life when he is alone, he does not belong in the pastorate. If he is the kind of person who needs to have a committee to keep him in line, he will end up bringing grief to the church."[52]

---

[51] Allen, *Discerning Your Call*, 35.
[52] Taken from transcript of John MacArthur's sermon, "The Qualifications for a Pastor, Part 2; Noble Character, Part 2," on December 13, 1992, accessed February 4, 2017, https://www.gty.org/library/sermons-library/56-8/the-qualifications-for-a-pastor-part-2-noble-character-part-2.

The qualifications speak a great deal to the character of the pastor, but character leads to how the minister functions. The qualifications offer guidelines for the pastor to walk in wisdom, peace, and continued integrity.

Bisagno rightly declares that integrity is a non-negotiable characteristic in the life of the minister. He shares, "Integrity, and the lack thereof, might well be the most important issue in America today; certainly in the ministry"[53]

The need for integrity mandates that the minister pay special attention to several particular areas of his behavior. There are many personality traits that are valuable for the minister, but one is indispensable. Again, Bisagno affirms, "You don't have to be highly educated, talented, or attractive to be greatly used of God, but you have to have integrity."[54]

Iorg brings another insight into the conversation when he writes, "Some people caution against elevating pastors and expecting them to live exemplary lives. The Bible indicates otherwise. Pastors are expected to live differently, to be above reproach."[55]

Therefore an overseer must be above reproach ... husband of one wife

Except for the grace of God ...

These are the words that come to my heart and mind when I hear the story of a minister failing morally. The world seems to rejoice when this happens, while it is certain that the Christian world should grieve.

The story is too often repeated; a gifted minister gets wrapped up in an immoral relationship, deals unethically with money, or

---

[53]Bisagno, *The Pastor's Handbook*, 105.
[54]Ibid., 106.
[55]Iorg, *Is God Calling Me*, 106.

gets caught in spoken lies and other types of dishonesty. I believe most do not begin their ministries with these types of moral flaws, but over the course of time, they grow stale in their love for the Savior and begin to make small compromises that lead to life-altering mistakes.

The following pages present and interact with some of the pitfalls that the pastor must avoid. Some are obvious, and others are much less obvious but, in many ways, just as dangerous. The two most obvious pitfalls that ministers must avoid are inappropriate relationships with the opposite sex and the mishandling of money.

I have one simple piece of advice when it comes to women and money: Never touch anybody's but your own!

I say it this way to get people's attention and maybe draw a laugh, but I am completely serious, as well. How a minister relates to the opposite sex is pivotal.

The following are certain rules that I strive to always follow in guarding my relationships with women for the sake of my witness, the health of my marriage, and for the protection of the people and institutions for which I am an ambassador. As you read these guidelines, some of you might argue that I am too uptight. But that's fine; if somebody does not think you are too uptight in this area, then you are likely not guarded enough.

Never be alone with a woman other than your wife. Not in your office, not in a restaurant, not at the coffee shop, not in an automobile, not in a home. I try not to even get on the elevator alone with a woman. I am convinced that if I am never alone with another woman, I will never have an inappropriate relationship with a woman who is not my wife.

Guard against emotional bonding by you or others to you. We must be careful in how we answer phone calls, emails, social media, texts and so forth. It is not proper for you to have extended communication with a woman other than your wife through any of these mediums. Additionally, your wife should have unfettered access to all of them. If she does not, what are you hiding?

Be very careful with outward affection. Learn the "side hug" technique. There is no one on the planet who gets a voluntary face-to-face hug from me except for my wife. There certainly is a place for physical contact; however, we must always remain above reproach. Your wife is a great gift in this area. Many times, I have prayed over a lady with a hand on her shoulder while my wife embraced her.

Do not discuss your marital issues with a woman. Do pastors ever have marital issues that they may need to discuss with someone? Certainly, but seek out the godly counsel of a brother in Christ. It is unfathomable to me that someone would not see the problem with sharing such intimate details with another woman, and yet I hear of this happening even amongst pastors.

Guard against the adulterous woman. Some may find what I am about to write offensive, but I believe it to be absolutely true. I believe most every church has a woman who, given opportunity, would cause the pastor to fail morally. Proverbs is clear: We must guard against the adulterous woman, and many times, she is not outside the church fellowship, but inside.

Avoid pornography in the same manner. The widespread problem of pornography is not getting the rebuke and attention that it needs. The ease with which someone can view such filth in our day is scary, to say the least. I am convinced that a man who has not gained consistent victory in this area is unqualified to serve in the office of pastor.

Allen exhorts, "Those who regularly digest pornography are unfit for ministry. If you find yourself struggling to some degree with pornography, you should discuss this with your pastor and others who are helping you discern your call to ministry."[56] Get victory in this area before it wreaks destruction on your life, family, and those you serve.

Never be alone with a woman other than your wife. I know I already said this, but it bears repeating. Guard yourself; the

---

[56]Allen, *Discerning Your Call*, 51.

moment you think you are invincible to these types of temptations is when you are likely in the most danger.

One final word: Trust your wife's instincts on these issues. I do not claim to understand it, but ladies have a radar for these things. If your wife warns you to be on guard concerning a certain woman, you would be wise to heed her advice, and foolish and without excuse if you do not.

Over our thirteen years of marriage, I remember two very clear warnings from my wife, and both of the women about whom she warned me were exposed in extramarital affairs within a year of my wife's warnings concerning them. TRUST YOUR WIFE'S INSTINCTS!

One particular interpretation of the "husband of one wife" phrase in the qualifications must at least be mentioned before continuing. There are many who use this phrase to say that a man who has been divorced is disqualified from the office of pastor. I would offer that the greater evidence to such a stance is found in the language of 1 Timothy 3 demanding that the elder must "manage his own family well" (verse 4). This discussion will be covered in greater detail when we get to the pastor and his family in chapter 4.

Every semester, when I talk to my students about the many pitfalls that ministers need to avoid, I ask them to name the most dangerous areas where a minister could make a catastrophic mistake. Inevitably, the number one answer is some sort of sexual sin. As we continue the conversation, especially if I ask them to give examples of reasons why someone could be fired or asked to resign from a ministry position, the next common answer is the mishandling of money.

Therefore an overseer must be above reproach ... not greedy for money

In 1 Timothy 6:9-10, Paul writes, "Those who want to get rich fall into temptation and a trap and into many foolish and harmful desires that plunge people into ruin and destruction. For the love of money is a root of all kinds of evil. Some people, eager for money, have wandered from the faith and pierced themselves with many griefs."

One of the qualifications for the pastor is that he should not be "greedy for money" or "covetous." Covetousness can refer to the desire for anything that someone else has, but the word is a combination of two words in the original language meaning "love of silver." The minister has to have a right attitude, practice, and understanding of money. He must give vision and leadership in financial decisions, be a good steward of his own financial resources, and teach the saints to do the same.

Here are five principles that ministers should follow when it comes to personal and church finances:

1. Be above reproach in personal finances. The biblical qualifications in 1 Timothy 3 require pastors be above reproach. How can you be above reproach in your finances? The main way is to pay your bills on time. Have integrity to meet the financial promises that you have made to those with whom you do business.

2. Be wise in handling church money. Never spend money where you have not been explicitly authorized to do so. And even when authorized, keep detailed records. I suggest you make copies of the receipts that you turn in and keep an electronic copy, as well. Strive to make it obvious that you are above reproach with church finances.

In my opinion, you are absolutely crazy if you or anyone in your family agrees to serve as church treasurer. There are just too many opportunities for issues and accusations when a pastor or family member serves in this type of leadership. We should cast vision for the use of church finances but not be in charge of the recordkeeping.

3. Avoid debt. Too many pastors are so swallowed up in personal debt that they are more concerned with their finances than with the ministry to which God has called them. I encourage every pastor to avoid any debt except for a house. Why do I do this? I have learned the hard way how credit card debt as well as student and auto loans can enslave the pastor and rob him of peace and power. I strongly recommend the resources at www.crown.org and www.daveramsey.com to those who need help in this area.

4. Don't live above the average level of your congregation. We must avoid legalism in this area, but we must also stay above reproach and avoid even the appearance of evil—that is, avoid looking like we are greedy for money or, my favorite translation, "filthy lucre." I think it wise for the pastor to maintain a lifestyle that falls close to the median income of his congregation. You do not need to live like the poorest, but you probably should not have a lifestyle equivalent to the richest member either. Ultimately, we must seek God's discernment in this area.

5. Be careful when leading a church into substantial debt. "God has called us to build a new building, and we need to step out on faith." "We NEED more space, and God is leading us to build." We must be careful when we claim God's leading in any area. Many times, God gets blamed for building projects that He had nothing to do with.

There are a few specific rules that I embrace in this area. First, building debt should never be at a level where it hinders ministry. Many churches become so shackled by debt that it greatly hinders their ability to do ministry at home and around the world.

Second, as a pastor, if you feel led of God to take a church into substantial debt, then have the integrity to lead them out of it. I am amazed how many times I hear a pastor has led a church into substantial debt, claiming God's will in the matter, just to turn around and feel "led" to a larger church across the state. I would contend that they quite possibly missed the will of God in one or both matters.

Third, if you inherit debt as a pastor, passionately lead your church to get out of debt quicker than scheduled. Fourth, wait to build until you have a substantial amount of the money on hand, preferably half or more of the total projected cost. Do not give up on the fact that building projects can be paid for without any debt whatsoever. It is not difficult to find numerous stories of how churches have been incredibly blessed to build as they go and learn to trust God in the process.

Finally, if you do borrow money, strive to borrow with the goal of being out of debt in three years or less. I have been amazed how quickly churches can pay off substantial debt in a quick period of time when they are challenged to do so!

Remember, money is amoral—it is neither good nor evil—but how we use it can either glorify God and advance His Kingdom or cause people to stumble. Let us be good stewards of all that God has entrusted to us in our personal lives and in the ministries we oversee.

Other Tips for Maintaining Integrity

Therefore an overseer must be above reproach ... sober-minded, just, holy, self-controlled

Many of the qualifications for the man who would seek the office of pastor can be summarized as his need to consistently display the fruit of the Spirit. The qualifications give many positive qualities that should be consistently present, as well as several negative qualities that should be consistently absent. The following are some reminders for pastors to help them continue in the state of being qualified for such a high calling.

Pastors must be real. We already spoke of integrity and the absolute need for it in the ministry. We have to exhibit a genuine walk with Christ before the body, and we "must have a good reputation with those outside the church" (1 Timothy 3:7). Bisagno defines integrity as "doing what people assume a man of God does when nobody's looking."[57]

Don't fall into the trap of God-given talents. Any gift we have comes from God, but such gifts can be used for His glory or exploited for personal gain and/or praise. The reality is that if you walk with God in genuine obedience, He is going to use you to

---

[57]Bisagno, *Pastor's Handbook*, 106.

glorify Himself. Most likely, He is going to use you in ways you never thought possible. It is an amazing privilege to see God work in such amazing ways. The trouble comes when we begin to think we really had anything to do with it!

Don't try to be what you are not, but be a pure you. You are not the next Billy Graham, Adrian Rogers, John MacArthur, Matt Chandler, David Platt, or [insert whatever Christian hero you wish to emulate]. God created you to be you, to walk in obedience to Him. The greatest person you can be for the Kingdom is you under the control of the Holy Spirit.

Don't be overly concerned with the crowd, but pay attention to the individual. As the pastor, it is imperative that you love people, but it needs to be clear that you love the individual, as well. For this reason, you need more often than not to show up early and stay late. Make sure you are not in a hurry with people, and as much as possible, take your time. Pay attention to the person to whom you are speaking, make eye contact, and avoid the temptation to be looking for bigger/better or even the next person. It is better to have three or four meaningful conversations than twenty empty ones.

Be aware of the trap of pride. As a pastor, you must always have a teachable spirit, never thinking more highly of yourself than you ought (Romans 12:3–5). Be careful not to believe your own headlines, whether they be good or bad. The reality is that you are probably not as good as your best headlines and not as bad as your worst. Strive to please God and not chase after the approval of people.

Constantly sharpen your people skills. The greatest motivation in tending the sheep is having a genuine love for them. Be reminded that it never hurts to give a kind, gentle response in tough situations (Proverbs 15:1). Make sure to guard your tongue, even amongst friends. Guard your keyboard, as well. There is little to be gained in trying to be cute or win arguments on social media.

The pastor should stay at peace if at all possible. Avoid conflict without compromising truth. There is something to be commended about the man who can agree to disagree without being disagreeable.

Conclusion

The pastor is qualified by Christ and his obedience to Christ's command. The pastor is motivated by his call and opportunity to serve amongst countless needs. He is compelled in his service by a genuine love for the sheep.

Bisagno asks a penetrating question: "Do I see people as an object, a prize to be won, a statistic to be added that my denominational paper might write an article about my growing church, enticing a larger church to call me as pastor? Or, do I see people as sheep in need of a shepherd?"[58]

---

[58]Bisagno, *Pastor's Handbook*, 60.

Chapter 4

Time for Your Primary Ministry:
"One who rules his household well"

The title of this book is *Everyday Ministry*, and to this point, the focus has been on the character and call of the minister. In some ways, we now turn our attention to the day-to-day function of the minister, although much function flows from character.

The previous chapters dealt with a continual state of being—the importance of walking daily with Jesus, trusting in your call, and walking in integrity alone and before the world. As we turn our attention to the practice of ministry, each of the subjects we will cover actually consumes the time of the minister on a daily, frequent, or occasional basis.

As ministers, we must be reminded that our primary ministry is at home. The qualifications in 1 Timothy 3 and Titus 1 make it clear that a man must give evidence of ministering to his family before he can be considered qualified for the office of pastor.

There is great pressure and scrutiny on the life and family of the pastor. For this reason, the qualifications are very clear that the pastor should have a solid testimony in the area of leading his family well. Both qualification passages require that the pastor be the "husband of one wife." There are many arguments surrounding this phrase, and space does not allow the opportunity to chase each of these.[59] However, the clear teaching absolutely includes that the pastor must be a man who gives evidence of being faithful and true to his wife. He must be a man of integrity in his marital relationship.

Though we could spend the rest of this volume and many more arguing the issue, I feel strongly that a man who has gone through the tragedy of divorce is not qualified to serve in the office of pastor. Forgiveness and restoration are certainly attainable, but the testimony of divorce declares to the world a failure to lead one's family well. Such a conclusion is often viewed as harsh or ungracious, but this was long the common view on the subject, and much yielding has more to do with the culture in which we live than with faithful understanding of the text.

Wayne Oates summarizes the issue well:

This is not to say that a divorced person cannot find vocation of Christian helpfulness to people and serve as a faithful witness to Christ. Nor is this to say that anything other than a spirit of gentle restoration should be used in counseling such a man. It is to say, however, that Christian compassion for the man himself as well as reverent concern for the New Testament standards of the ministry call for a man who has made a success of his first marriage.[60]

The qualifications also speak about the pastor's children. Paul declares to Titus that a man desiring to be a pastor must have "children who believe, not accused of dissipation or rebellion" (Titus 1:6). Paul gives even more detail to Timothy when he writes that a pastor must be "one who manages his own household well, keeping his children under control with all dignity" (1 Timothy 3:4). The

---

[59]For a concise commentary on the qualifications in Titus, see Paige Patterson, *Living in Hope of Eternal Life: An Exposition of the Book of Titus* (Eugune, OR: Wipf & Stock, 1968).

[60]Wayne Oates, *The Christian Pastor* (Philadelphia, PA: Westminster Press, 1951), 48.

idea is that a man who desires to pastor the flock of God must first show that he is able to pastor his family.

It becomes even more evident that this is Paul's meaning when he adds in verse 5, "but if a man does not know how to manage his own household, how will he take care of the church of God?" The minister must first and primarily minister to his family. He must already be doing this in order to be qualified for the office of pastor, and he must continue doing this if he is to remain in such an office.

John MacArthur explains why the qualifications concerning the pastor are so strong in the New Testament. He writes, "The New Testament certainly does not ignore the potentially severe pressures of the ministry. However, it does demand the kinds of men and the kinds of families for ministry that can successfully avoid the damage that would surely come to the marriage and/or family of one who does not have a strong commitment to comply with the biblical standards."[61] He continues, "God anticipated the unusual demands on the pastor's home by requiring that a potential pastor already have a strong commitment in these areas *before* he qualifies for ministry."[62]

The minister must effectively pastor his own family before he can pastor the family of God. He must also remain consistent in such a testimony of "managing his own household well." What does this look like? There are so many ideas and tangents that could be discussed, but at the risk of oversimplifying the issue, LOVE YOUR FAMILY!

Loving and leading your family means they are a priority, they receive your attention, you are intentional to guard your time with them, and you concern yourself greatly with their spiritual needs. My observation of some ministers is that they neglect their families for the sake of other ministry. God has not called us to sacrifice our family on the altar of ministry. Paul even wrote that "If anyone does not provide for his own, and especially for those of his household,

---

[61]MacArthur, *Pastoral Ministry: How to Shepherd Biblically*, 123.
[62]Ibid., 130 (emphasis added).

he has denied the faith and is worse than an unbeliever" (1 Timothy 5:8).

I have also seen the minister use his family as an excuse to neglect ministry. There is a balance, and I wish I could give you an easy way to figure it out for your family, but you have an obligation to figure it out if you desire to remain qualified for the office of pastor. The remainder of this chapter shares tips that I have found helpful in trying to navigate such a difficult but worthwhile path.

Steps Taken by the Wise Pastor in Regard to Family

Set aside time each week to be with your wife. Give her specific, intentional, and undivided attention at some point every week. Make time with her; turn off the television, the iPad, the laptop; and have a real conversation.

Ask her how her day went and listen. Listen more than you really want to listen. You know what I am talking about. When we ask, "How was your day?" we want to listen to a ten-second or less response. Your wife probably needs to give you more information. She desires and, in many ways, needs to be heard. You might also want to give her specific information when she asks about your day.

Do not forget to keep dating your wife. Take your wife out to dinner without the children. Budget money for a babysitter. You do not have to go somewhere fancy, but she would probably appreciate if it were somewhere quiet and without any sports on television. If money is an issue, just go for a quick walk around the neighborhood together or go to free places like museums or anything she may enjoy. Take time to minister to the needs of your wife by setting aside specific time for her.

Set aside time each week to be with your children. If you have children, you know for a fact that they grow up way too fast. They are going to be gone and out of the house before you realize it. Do you want them to leave thinking (a) their dad was always too busy to spend time with them, or (b) their dad was busy, but he always took time to spend with them?

You are going to be busy, but make time to spend with your children together as a family. I would also encourage you to take individual time with each child on a consistent and meaningful basis.

Eat at least one meal a day together. What happened to the family sitting around the table together and sharing a meal? We live in a busy culture today, and the minister's family has even more added to the schedule. On top of the busyness, we often fail to even turn off the television and actually have conversation when we do eat together. There are going to be days when it just is not possible, but strive to eat at least one meal together every day as a family.

Have a consistent, age-appropriate family devotion. If you are going to effectively pastor your family, you have to spend time in worship together. A simple time of reading Scripture, sharing prayer concerns, singing a song or two, and praying together is a sweet blessing and instills in your family a deeper love for one another and for our Lord Jesus. Our family used to try and do this right before bed, and that is certainly an acceptable time if it works for you and your family.

We found that time difficult to maintain with evening activities at church, school, and sports practices, however. There were many times we did not get home until at or past bedtime, so we would rush to get showers and get through the worship time. Many nights, it was a quick prayer and included somebody fussing more often than I would like to admit.

So, we have combined the importance of the family meal with our worship time. We spend most evening meals together, and before we leave the table, we have our family devotion. There are still plenty of nights when there are other appointments after supper, but it is much easier to make time before we leave than try to find it at the end of the day.

I can testify that this is one of my favorite times of the day—sitting at the table with my family. I love being with them, I love reading through Scripture and praying, and I love to eat! (My wife is a great cook.) Just do whatever works best for your family.[63]

Pray with your wife personally on a consistent basis. One of the greatest blessings you can give your wife is to pray with her on a consistent basis. Certainly, in tough times and obvious struggles, you should minister to and with your wife in prayer. But you should also pray for her on a daily basis, many times a day.

You should pray together every day as a family, but do not let family prayer time replace the intimacy of prayer together with your mate and ministry partner. Look your wife in the eyes, tell her you love her, and ask her to share with you how and what you can pray about in her life. Then take her by the hands and cry out to God on her behalf. I believe this is one of the most effective ways—if not the most effective way—to minister to your wife's heart.

Always attend children's extracurricular activities. I am the son of a Southern Baptist pastor. I loved being a preacher's kid; I felt like I got to do things that the rest of the children at church missed out on. I could play in the graveyard without getting in trouble, for example; it was part of the yard outside the house where I grew up.

My dad is a great man of God, loves Jesus, faithfully served as a pastor for more than 35 years, and continues to serve churches as an interim pastor. He was always busy, and the churches he served involved a lot of pastoral care, trips to hospitals, and time away from us to do what God called him to do.

Even with the long hours and busy schedule, one thing I remember with great gratitude is that when I had a ball game, a tennis match, a golf tournament, or some other event, Dad was there. I am sure there were a few times when he could not make it, but I do not remember any of them. What I do remember is that there

---

[63]For more on the importance and practice of family worship, see "Spiritual Formation through Family Worship: The Heart of the Matter" by Malcolm and Karen Yarnell in *Everyday Parenting* (ed. Alex Sibley (Fort Worth, TX: Seminary Hill Press, 2017), 53-66).

was no doubt in my mind that my dad supported me and made me a priority in his schedule.

As a minister, you need to put your children's activities on the calendar as a high-level, important event, and guard those appointments diligently. It ought to grieve you if something causes you to miss one of your children's activities.

Now with that said, use wisdom in how many activities your children take on. Our culture leans toward absurdity when it comes to what our children HAVE to take part in. Make sure your children always know God is everything, family second, church a close third, and everything else finds its place after that!

Take meaningful vacations where you are present. Be sure to take the vacation that the church you serve allows you to take. There is nothing spiritual in never taking meaningful rest. Quite the opposite, such a practice is sinful and ignores Sabbath principles. I would encourage you to take vacations that actually leave you rested. Sometimes we over-plan our travel and come back more tired than when we left.

Be present on vacation—not just physically, but mentally as well. Leave the laptop at the office, use the iPad for pictures, turn off the notifications on your phone, and ENJOY resting and being with your family.

Do ministry together. Ministry is filled with activities, and many of those activities require the pastor to be away from his family. There are many times, however, when the minister is able to take his wife and even his children on ministry assignments.

There were several senior adults and shut-ins who would get upset with me if my wife and children were not with me on the visit. I am fairly certain many of them would rather see them than me, and we enjoyed our time together. It also gave opportunity for our children to see how we love one another, and for the church members to see their pastor on a truly human level.

The principle here should be thought about for the entire church, as well. Be intentional to plan ministry that helps the family do ministry together and grow together.

Guard your time with your family. The minister should treat time with family like any other extremely important appointment. There are things that cannot be avoided, but very little should interrupt time (ministry) with your family.

Make sure your wife has considerable input in your calendar. I made my calendar available on my wife's phone so she gets a reminder for each of my appointments. She loves this, and it is a blessing to her.

Communicate your schedule clearly to your family and to the church you serve. If you have specific times each week that you desire to guard for family time, let your church know so they can help you in that endeavor.

The minister should establish an understanding with his wife and a policy with his primary ministry concerning outside speaking engagements and vacations/days off. You do not have policies with your wife, so you come to an agreement, but with your wife and ministry, communication is the key to guarding a healthy balance between your obligation to your family and other ministry. You and your wife need to budget your time at least once monthly, preferably weekly and even daily on some level, with openness to whatever level of communication is necessary.

Think through your "off" time. There are certainly a lot of activities that a pastor could be involved in during his "off" time such as golf, travel, or any other hobby. He may want to participate in a community service organization or some other club. The key is to think through the time investment and the season of life your children and family are experiencing. Ministers may be tempted to flop down in front of the television or some other electronic device every evening. We need to consider the value that our time spent adds or subtracts from how we "manage our household."

Oswald Sanders argues that we often have more time than we admit. He points out that if we allot ourselves a generous eight hours of sleep per day, ten hours for work and travel, and three hours for meals, that still leaves over twenty hours a week to fill. What happens to those hours? He argues, "A person's entire contribution to the kingdom of God may turn on how those hours are used. Certainly those hours determine whether life is commonplace or extraordinary."[64]

A good investment of many of those hours should go toward the pastor's family. Heed the words of long-time pastor John Bisagno: "Family first! You can always find someone to help you do the work of the church, but no one can love your wife and raise your children except you."[65] Pastor, do not get thirty years down the road and realize you lost your most important ministry, your wife and children.

---

[64]J. Oswald Sanders, *Spiritual Leadership: Principles of Excellence for Every Believer* (Chicago, IL: Moody, 2007), 95.
[65]Bisagno, *The Pastor's Handbook*, 62.

Chapter 5

Time for the Study:
"Able to teach ... holding fast"

The qualifications are clear that the pastor must be able to teach, holding fast the Word with sound doctrine. Though some would disagree, I believe the primary task of any pastor is his preaching/teaching ministry. Allen argues, "A call to preach or teach the Word is the distinguishing mark of a call to the ministry."[66] Charles Spurgeon's lecture on discerning a call to ministry makes such a call nearly synonymous with the call to preach.

A clear message of Scripture is a heavy burden and a stricter judgment placed on those who teach the Word. James 3:1 states, "Let not many of you become teachers, my brethren, knowing that as such we will incur a stricter judgment." The thought of a stricter judgment should persuade anyone not to enter the task of preaching in his own strength.

Furthermore, Hebrews 13:7 states, "Remember those who led you, who spoke the word of God to you; and considering the result of their conduct, imitate their faith." Later in the same passage, the Scripture continues, "Obey your leaders and submit to them, for they keep watch over your souls as those who will give an account. Let them do this with joy and not with grief, for this would be unprofitable for you" (verse 17). These are sobering reminders that

---

[66] Allen, *Discerning Your Call*, 22.

the pastor must take the task of preaching/teaching the Word with the greatest of seriousness.

A key aspect to remember is that sermon preparation is labor. It certainly should be an enjoyable labor, a labor of love, but it is labor. J.H. Jowett contends, "Preaching that costs nothing accomplishes nothing. If the study is a lounge the pulpit will be an impertinence. It is, therefore, imperative that the preacher go into his study to do hard work."[67]

The preaching moment is normally the opportunity to make the greatest impact with the largest number of people in your congregation. For this reason, Draper urges, "Your congregation will most easily receive your word as you preach, so being prepared to share is your first priority of service to them."[68]

Sermon Preparation

Time spent in sermon preparation is probably going to be and should be the greatest expenditure of your time from week to week. There are always going to be sermons and weekly lessons to prepare. Most pastors are going to preach or teach at least two or three times per week. It has been the experience of many that any pastor should plan on at least fifteen to twenty hours per week in the study and preparation of sermons.

Preaching is one of the primary tasks by which the pastor feeds, protects, and trains the sheep. One wonderful truth about the diligent study of Scripture is that it also prepares you for all the other day-to-day tasks of the pastor.

There will be times when you get overwhelmed by the limitless tasks of the ministry and will be tempted to neglect the study. Stott reminds the pastor, "The systematic preaching of the Word is impossible without the systematic *study* of it."[69] Jay Adams laments,

---

[67]Jowett, *The Preacher*, 114.
[68]Draper, *Don't Quit Before You Finish*, 54.
[69]John Stott, *The Preacher's Portrait: Some New Testament Word Studies* (Grand Rapids, MI: Eerdmans, 1988), 31.

"I am convinced that the basic reason for poor preaching is the failure to spend adequate time and energy in preparation."[70] Always remember that the study of the Word is what most effectively equips you for all the other tasks.

Heed this exhortation if you remember or follow nothing else in this entire work. Determine from the very beginning to preach and teach "thus saith the Lord" from the inspired, inerrant, infallible Scripture.

The members of the flock do not need another self-help guide, feel-good preacher, or prosperity message. They desperately need to hear from God and what He has spoken through His Word. MacArthur argues such a commitment goes "beyond a commitment to its inspiration and inerrancy, it also entails a commitment to its absolute authority and sufficiency."[71]

There is not enough space in the scope of this work to give a full treatment of sermon preparation and how to divide each particular text, but the following is a very basic outline for sermon preparation.[72] For further study, I would highly recommend the three following works:

> Daniel Akin, David Allen, and Ned Matthews, eds. *Text-Driven Preaching: God's Word at the Heart of Every Sermon*. Nashville, TN: Broadman & Holman, 2010.
>
> Wayne McDill. *Twelve Essential Skills for Great Preaching*. Nashville, TN: Broadman & Holman, 2010.
>
> Jerry Vines and Jim Shaddix. *Power in the Pulpit: How to Prepare and Deliver Expository Sermons*. Chicago, IL: Moody, 2017.

Saturate your preparation in prayer. In Acts 6, the apostles determine that it is not suitable for them to neglect the study of the Word in order to wait on tables. What we often neglect when

---

[70]Jay Adams, "Editorial: Good Preaching is Hard Work," *The Journal of Pastoral Practice* 4, no. 2 (1980), 1.
[71]MacArthur, *Pastoral Ministry: How to Shepherd Biblically*, 208.
[72]For sermon preparation resources, semantic layout of biblical passages, and schedules of preaching conferences and workshops, see www.preachingsource.com.

remembering this passage is that it also highlights prayer—"But we will devote ourselves to prayer and to the ministry of the word" (Acts 6:4). Spurgeon encourages the pastor in prayer: "You will frequently find fresh streams of thought leaping from the passage before you, as if the rock had been struck by Moses' rod; new veins of precious ore will be revealed to your astonished gaze as you quarry God's Word and use diligently the hammer of prayer."[73]

Gain a concise understanding of the main point of the passage. One of the most primary tasks—if not the most primary task—in the preparation of any sermon is gaining a clear understanding of the main point of the text. Jowett clearly came to the same conclusion. He wrote, "I have a conviction that no sermon is ready for preaching, not ready for writing out, until we can express its theme in a short, pregnant sentence as clear as a crystal."[74] Make sure you can explain the overarching message of the sermon in a simple and memorable sentence.

Discern principles from the passage. Make sure that you pull your main points from the text. Do not get caught up in trying to have a certain number of points or get caught in the trap of trying to alliterate everything. If you have to use a thesaurus to find a word that starts with the right letter, chances are it will be lost on your audience. The sermon outline should be memorable and divisible, but the text is able to accomplish both of these.

> **Explain the principle.** The most important part of any sermon is sharing what the text says. The preacher must be sure to stay faithful in explaining what the Scripture actually says rather than his opinion of it. The greatest detail work is done in this area with translating the text from the original language and doing substantial word studies.
>
> **Argue the principle.** Through argumentation, we provide evidence of the truth of the principle. The greatest commentary on the Scripture is Scripture itself. The warning in this work is to make sure that we use cross references from

---

[73]Spurgeon, *Lectures to My Students*, 44.
[74]Jowett, *The Preacher*, 133.

passages with similar contexts. We do not want to fall into the trap of proof-texting.

Illustrate the principle. Many preachers spend an inordinate amount of time trying to craft the perfect illustrations, and yet others neglect the value of illustrating the text. Timely, valid, and honest illustrations can shed great understanding on the text and lead to more clear application. However, we need to guard against the illustrations overshadowing the text itself. Be sure not to miss the many times that helpful illustrations are actually in the text itself.

Apply the principle. Finally, the preacher needs to help the audience understand what the response to the message should be. One of the primary ways to glean the application of a text is to recognize the imperatives found in the passage. When determining the application for each principle, the preacher also recognizes crucial aspects for the invitation. Many times, preachers develop canned invitations that have little impact or are dangerously manipulative. Just as every sermon should be text-driven, so should the invitation. Certainly, every invitation should include a plea for the Gospel, but the primary application of the text provides an important part of the invitation.

Use varying levels of commentaries. There is a nearly limitless number of commentaries available on every book of the Bible. The temptation looms to quickly turn to the commentaries and allow them to shape the bulk of the sermon. However, I would encourage the preacher to develop the structure and content of the sermon first, and then consult the commentaries to refine and add clarity to the sermon.

Commentaries contain an abundance of material that helps explain, argue, illustrate, and apply the text. The following may be an oversimplification, but commentaries can be divided into three major categories. It is not that one category is better than the others, but each category offers certain benefits toward sermon preparation.

Sermonic: Commentaries placed in this category are quite simply sermons that have been published. There is a great benefit in reading sermons by others on the passage you are preaching. There can be valuable insight gleaned for all areas of the sermon. Again, you want to have the main body of your sermon prepared before consulting commentaries so you are not tempted to just preach someone else's message.

Theological: These types of commentaries expound the main theological themes found in the passage. There normally is pertinent background and historical material. These types of commentaries also provide insight into the author, recipients, provenance, and other important facets of the passage.

Exegetical: The main characteristic of this category is the inclusion of critical work with the original languages.

To have at least two or three commentaries from each category when preparing sermons is helpful. The availability of many works through Bible software is extremely advantageous in our day of sermon preparation. Such software makes for a great investment to the toolkit of any preacher.[75] There really is no excuse not to put in the diligent work to prepare quality sermons.

The following sources will help you in locating quality commentaries from varying categories:

David Allen. *Preaching Tools: An Annotated Survey of Commentaries and Preaching Resources for Every Book of the Bible*, revised 2nd ed. Fort Worth, TX: Seminary Hill Press, 2017.

Daniel Akin. *Building a Theological Library*. http://www.danielakin.com/building-a-theological-library-2013-update/

D.A. Carson. *Best Commentaries*. http://bestcommentaries.com/

Prepare multiple sermons at a time. Below, arguments are made for why preaching through books of the Bible produces the

---

[75]There are many Bible software plans available. The more popular and, in my opinion, most helpful are: www.logos.com, www.accordancebible.com, and www.bibleworks.com.

most effective study time for the preacher. One additional reason requires explanation here. As mentioned above, a pastor can easily spend fifteen to twenty hours a week in the study preparing sermons. I always found it beneficial to be working on several sermons at once. The more sermons you prepare, the more adept you become in putting together the primary structures of a sermon.

Preachers may find it helpful to lay sermons aside several times during the preparation process and come back to them with a fresh look. Preaching through entire books of the Bible provides great synergy in sermon preparation and an ease of working on several sermons through the entire book simultaneously.

Make sure the text has spoken to you. The task of preparing sermons is laborious. However, it must be a spiritual task, as well. You are not ready to preach a text until it has burned in your heart as the preacher.

John Owens exclaims, "I therefore hold myself bound in conscience and in honor, not even to imagine that I have attained a proper knowledge of any one article of truth, much less to publish it, unless through the Holy Spirit I have had such a taste of it, in its spiritual sense, that I may be able from the heart to say with the psalmist, 'I have believed and therefore have spoken.'"[76]

Remove yourself from distractions in the moments before preaching. You have labored over the sermon, done the technical exegesis, laid out the outline, developed timely and impactful illustrations, prepared clear and text-driven applications, and you are ready to preach the message. On the way to the sanctuary, you are bombarded by three people complaining about everything from the temperature to their Sunday School teacher. Two others demand you make announcements for some random event, and others have legitimate concerns that need hours, not seconds, to handle.

The tasks of the pastor are nearly countless, and often such interruptions are unavoidable, but the preacher needs to be still and in-step with God before he enters the pulpit. Spurgeon suggests the preacher get alone with God before taking the pulpit. He writes,

---

[76]John Owen, *Sin & Temptation* (Portland, MA: Multnomah, 1983), xviii.

"Prayer will singularly assist you in the delivery of your sermon; in fact, nothing can so gloriously fit you to preach as descending fresh from the mount of communion with God to speak with men."[77]

There are many times when it is nearly impossible to avoid interruptions, but great effort should be made to ensure that the last thought of the preacher before entering the pulpit is his sermon and the great God it glorifies.

The Best Way to Preach is Through Books of the Bible

Serving at Southwestern Baptist Theological Seminary, where we espouse what is called "text-driven preaching," is a joy. Simply put, we want the chosen text (yes, there should be an actual biblical text) to drive the sermon. The text-driven preacher is committed to the content and structure of the text and attempts to communicate it faithfully to the hearer. I am convinced that this type of preaching produces the greatest benefit in any pastoral ministry setting.[78]

If you have been called to pastor, one of your main assignments is the week-by-week preaching and teaching of the Word of God. The overwhelming content of your preaching should be text-driven expository messages through books or major portions of the Scripture.

There are several reasons why I believe the pastor and his ministry are strengthened by this type of preaching. Text-driven preaching through books of the Bible:

Provides accountability and efficiency. The pastor who is preaching through a book of the Bible has the benefit of knowing where he is heading in his preaching. He does not have to figure out what he is going to preach when he gets into the office

---

[77]Spurgeon, *Lectures to My Students*, 45.
[78]For a more thorough, though concise, exploration of text-driven preaching, see *A Pastor's Guide to Text-Driven Preaching* (Fort Worth, TX: Seminary Hill Press, 2016). This resource was written by members of Southwestern Seminary's School of Preaching faculty, including Dean David Allen and President of Southwestern Paige Patterson.

Monday morning. Additionally, the audience provides accountability, because they know where he is heading as well and are looking for answers.

Covers the whole counsel of the Word of God. If we are not careful, as preachers, we can get fixated on particular topics or popular subjects of the day. When you preach through books of the Bible, you cover the whole of Scripture—the fun passages, the easy-to-understand passages, the popular passages, AND the unpopular passages.

Preachers must be able to confront the tough issues of the culture, even though some argue we should never be controversial. John Stott argues, "It is frequently said that pastors must always be positive in their teaching, never negative. But those who say this have either not read the New Testament or, having read it, they disagree with it. For the Lord Jesus and His apostles gave the example and even set forth the obligation to be negative in refuting error."[79]

Provides greater use of time. Preaching through a book of the Bible provides several areas where your time is used more efficiently. With numerous sermons from the same book, much of the work concerning context, background, provenance, audience, purpose of the work, and other details is dealt with from the beginning and takes less time in preparation each week.

Offers protection for the pastor. Have you ever preached a message because you were convinced a particular person needed to hear it? This is a dangerous method of choosing a sermon topic/text. An additional benefit of preaching through books is that it offers protection to the pastor. No one can claim, "He just picked that text because of what is going on in the church right now!" The reality is that we should be bold and preach truth no matter what the circumstance, but there is freedom and wisdom in trusting that God's Word can address church issues in God's timing.

Deals with all necessary issues. Sometimes, pastors lack patience, and we want to hit an issue head-on and have the exact text to do

---

[79]John Stott, "Ideals of Pastoral Ministry," in Roy Zuck, *Vital Ministry Issues: Examining Concerns and Conflicts in Ministry* (Eugene, OR: Wipf & Stock, 2004), 72.

it. I would argue that if you preach through books of the Bible, you can trust that the text eventually confronts all necessary issues, and normally with much better timing than we have on our own.

Provides ease in planning preaching and worship services. A very practical benefit to preaching through books is that it makes planning the preaching calendar much easier. I have found that music leaders like to know where the pastor is going, and when you are preaching through books of the Bible, it is much easier to plan worship services that actually have something to do with the sermon.

Feeds the body and encourages further study. Text-driven preaching through books of the Bible is a much healthier diet for the body of Christ. Preachers should consistently deliver faithful exposition of the text in a passionate and creative manner. I believe much of the unhealthiness in churches stems from an unhealthy diet from the pulpit.

Another interesting result of preaching through books of the Bible is that it increases questions concerning the biblical book. When I was preaching through the book of Daniel, while preaching in chapters 1–6, I was getting many questions about chapters 7–12. Are these types of questions and feedback beneficial to the preacher? I certainly thought so. I knew what types of questions my audience was asking about the text before I even preached the sermon. I did not incorporate all the questions into my content, but it certainly helped me better understand how to communicate to my audience.

Feeds the preacher. We are really not able to preach or teach a text until it has taught us. If you leave the study and head to the pulpit and the message has not gripped your soul, challenged your spirit, corrected your attitude, and caught fire in your being, you are not doing it right! The systematic day-to-day study of a book of the Bible is some of the most beneficial and rewarding time any pastor can spend. We are called to feed the sheep, but if we are not consuming the Word ourselves through diligent study, there is nothing to give.

In exhorting pastors to preach through books of the Bible, W.A. Criswell made this declaration,

> A remarkable thing happens when a pastor preaches through a book of the Bible. Too many preachers walk up and down their studies wringing their hands, crying "What shall I preach? And where can I get the pertinent material I need for my listening saints?"
>
> I also walk up and down my study, but my cry is altogether different. There is so much to preach, and so much God has said that I am afraid I am going to die before I have delivered the messages that I see in God's book.[80]

Delivery

You have labored all week in the study, preparing sermons so that you can teach and feed the family of God. Now it comes time to deliver the sermon. Here are just a few tips concerning the actual preaching event.

It should always be natural. Do not try to be someone else, and avoid being totally different in the pulpit than anywhere else. Just be yourself and lay aside "preacherisms" like a deeper voice or the need to quote authors whom no one in your congregation has ever heard of.

Make sure you are communicating the text. In your delivery, your main goal should be to communicate the text, not just give a motivational speech. Temptation may drive you to feverishly try to be on the cutting edge creatively. It is absolute fact that the sheep do not need our creativity as much as they need the Word of God explained. Focus on giving the text!

Preach your message without notes. By the time you preach a sermon, it should so indwell you and be so tied to the text that

---

[80]W.A. Criswell, *Criswell's Guidebook for Pastors* (Nashville, TN: Broadman Press, 1980), 61.

you can preach it rather easily without notes. In reality, text-driven preaching done correctly makes the text itself your notes.

Memorizing your material is beneficial for other reasons, as well. First, memorization gives confidence, authority, and freedom from being tied to notes on the pulpit. Second, memorization allows for greater eye contact, which grants greater connection with the audience. Third, memorization provides a much more natural delivery and connection with the audience in a conversational manner.

Extending the Invitation

There may be many forms of invitation, but every message should include an invitation. That is, every message should include some manner in which those who have received the Word can respond to the Word.

The invitation must never be extended in fleshly power but in the power of the Holy Spirit. Make sure that you do not just tag on to the end of every sermon some rote, vain, and repetitive invitation.

The invitation should be part of sermon preparation. Specifically, the invitation should include the primary application of the text. In text-driven preaching, we believe we should extend text-driven invitations. Every invitation is an invitation to the Gospel, for without the Gospel, we are incapable of responding in obedience to anything else.

The invitation should not be manipulative, high-pressured, too long, or confusing. If you are able to talk someone into something, life and trials can quickly talk them out of it.

I strongly believe that the one who preaches should extend the invitation. Again, the invitation is more than an extension of the sermon; it should be part of the sermon itself. Good invitations require thought in the sermon preparation and in the service planning. Do not be in a hurry to quickly close the invitation, but avoid unnecessarily extending it, as well.

Finally, at the conclusion of the service, do not be in a hurry to leave. Many times, people are touched by a biblically faithful sermon but then hesitate in responding publicly to the invitation. Often, those who linger following the service are waiting to discuss further what they heard in the message. Pay attention, and make a concerted effort to linger so they have opportunity to respond. Bryant and Brunson contend, "It could be that success in pastoral leadership rises or falls with how the pastor treats people when the church service is over."[81]

---

[81]Bryant and Brunson, *Guidebook for Pastors*, 106.

Chapter 6

With the Time that is Left ...
Prioritize for the Greatest Impact on the Kingdom

Time Management

As ministers, time is one of our most precious and often wasted resources. We must be diligent to guard and redeem our time, because there are always people and activities that desire to spend it.

Wondering Where Time Went

Do you remember thinking someone was just old when he/she said something like, "The older you get, the faster time goes"? Either I am just old, or age does not really have much to do with it.

I think, as we get older, we realize how precious time is, and we begin to understand its value. The Word of God shows the value and swiftness of time. Paul tells us to redeem the time because the days are evil (Ephesians 5:16; Colossians 4:5). James reminds us of the uncertainty of time when he exhorts his readers not to make plans without seeking the Lord and that our lives are but a vapor that appears for a little while and then vanishes (James 4:13–17). Job certainly recognized the swiftness and frailty of time (Job 9:25, 14:2)

A lot of people have more money or talent than I do, but nobody has more time. Time is the great equalizer; we all have twenty-four hours a day and seven days a week. Sanders maintains, "Our problem is not too little time but making better use of the time we have. Each of us has as much time as anyone else. The president of the United States has the same twenty-four hours as we. Others may surpass our abilities, influence, or money, but no one has more time."[82]

The difference, oftentimes, between glorifying the Lord in our lives and spiritual mediocrity is how we spend our time. Yes, I said "spend." Time is a commodity that we need to spend wisely.

Many start the New Year making all kinds of resolutions (concrete, measurable goals are a better route), and I would argue that how we use our time should receive significant attention. Dave Ramsey often says concerning money, "Tell your money where to go instead of wondering where it went." On that same note, we should "tell our time where to go instead of wondering where it went."

I want to deal with the "wondering where it went" portion of that phrase. (The next section presents several tips on how to "tell our time where to go.") A big step in guarding our time, redeeming the time, and creating more efficiency with our time is recognizing what I call "time-stealers."

Sleep. Of course, I am not saying you should not sleep. But how much sleep do you really need? Are you sleeping more than you should? Are you just lazy?

We have been told we need a solid eight hours of sleep a night, but many people can function just as well on six hours. Get the sleep you need, but get up and start the day. Proverbs speaks much about the dangers of too much sleep. We will spend close to a third of our lives sleeping, but let us not overdo it!

Television. A recent report showed that the average American watches somewhere between four and five hours of movies and TV shows per day![83] Think about this: the average American watches

---

[82]Sanders, *Spiritual Leadership*, 94.
[83]Jaqueline Howard, "Americans devote more than 10 hours a day to screen time, and

more than thirty hours of television per week, and more than 1,600 hours per year. Take that one step further over the course of a life-span of seventy years and the average American spends more than thirteen years of his life in front of a TV screen. Is this really "redeeming the time" or the best way to build the Kingdom? We have to avoid legalism, but we need to ask these questions.

Phones/Tablets. The same article shares that the average "screen" time for an American is more than ten hours per day. That means we spend nearly thirty years of our lives consuming media through screens. There is much content available that is edifying and redeeming, but we must guard against unredeemed time and pay attention to how our time is spent.

A few reminders:

- You do not have to respond every time your device makes a noise. Alerts can be muted or even turned off. The world will not end!
- Time spent endlessly scrolling through social media can most likely be used more effectively on some other activity.
- The makers of game apps are good at what they do and desire to get you "hooked" on their game.

Always avoid unwholesome or questionable content; it can never be redeeming. Paul writes, "Finally, brethren, whatever is true, whatever is honorable, whatever is right, whatever is pure, whatever is lovely, whatever is of good repute, if there is any excellence and if anything worthy of praise, dwell on these things" (Philippians 4:8).

Overscheduling. One final time-stealer that I would like to point out is that many of us just try to do too much! Sanders writes, "Often the pressure a spiritual leader feels comes from assuming tasks that God has not assigned. For such tasks the leader cannot expect God to supply the extra strength required."[84]

growing," June 30, 2016, accessed January 5, 2017, http://www.cnn.com/2016/06/30/health/americans-screen-time-nielsen/.
[84]Sanders, *Spiritual Leadership*, 97.

Many men and women overschedule their lives at work, at church, and even in their hobbies. Many families even add stress to their lives by overscheduling their children's extracurricular activities. There are many good and wholesome activities and even ministries, but God has not called us to participate in all of them.

Guard against these time-stealers; pay attention to where your time is going. We must seek to spend our time in the way that brings the greatest glory to our Father who is in heaven. The next section presents some tips for how to use the time we have more efficiently.

Tell Time Where to Go

I want to share with you a few tips I have gleaned and found helpful from a number of pastors that help "grow" more time by helping you be more efficient with the time you have.[85] These time-redeemers are geared toward men in pastoral ministry, but many of them can be applied to any career or line of work.

Find your security in Christ. We oftentimes overextend ourselves, not to please God but man. We need to understand that it is fine to say "no" as long as we have a more important task or assignment given from the Lord. Be gracious and kind, but labor for an audience of One!

Pray, pay attention, plan, and prioritize. The preacher in me could not help but group these four P's together.

> **Pray:** Obviously, we should start each day with prayer and Bible reading/devotion, but we should also pray and ask the Lord to guide our time through the day. Time is too important a commodity not to seek God's guidance concerning it.

---

[85]Much of the material given here is a summary of multiple sources on time management. The following were particularly helpful: John Bisagno, *Pastor's Handbook* (Nashville, TN: Broadman & Holman, 2011), 67–69; Johnny Hunt, *Building Your Leadership Resume: Developing the Legacy That Will Outlast You* (Nashville, TN: Broadman & Holman, 2009), 184–190; Nelson Searcy, *The Renegade Pastor: Abandoning Average in Your Life and Ministry* (Grand Rapids, MI: Baker, 2013), 85–102; Austin B. Tucker, *A Primer for Pastors: A Handbook for Strengthening Ministry Skills* (Grand Rapids, MI: Kregel, 2004), 173–201.

Pay attention: Many of us "leak" time during the day just because we do not pay attention. Watch where your time is going, what activities are distracting you and stealing your time, and limit them. At the very least, by paying attention, you can "plan" the distractions.

Plan: I believe that every family should do a monthly budget and review it often to be a good steward of financial resources. Likewise, we should spend a little time each day planning how we are going to spend our time. You might want to spend fifteen minutes or so at the end of each workday planning the "To Do List" for the next workday. When you walk in the office the next morning, you do not need to spend a lot of time figuring out what you should do!

Prioritize: Many times, the "urgent" tries to replace the "important." You need to prioritize what is most important and focus on that ONE task with intensity. Do not get distracted unless there is a genuine emergency. Strive to establish a weekly routine. There will be interruptions, but consistency breeds efficiency.

Start your day earlier. John Bisagno writes, "Expand your efficiency by expanding your morning."[86] If you get your day started at 6 a.m. instead of 8 a.m. five days a week, then you have an extra ten hours a week to get things done. Jowett shares a vivid illustration,

> Enter your study at the appointed hour, and let that hour be as early as the earliest of your business-men goes to his warehouse or his office. I remember my earlier days how I used to hear the factory operatives passing my house on the way to the mills where work began at six o'clock. I can recall the sound of their iron-clogs ringing through the street. The sound of the clogs fetched me out of bed and took me to my work.[87]

---

[86]Bisagno, *Pastor's Handbook*, 68.
[87]Jowett, *The Preacher*, 116.

How many of you would benefit from an extra ten hours? I understand you would be tired at night if you got up that early. Good! Go to bed earlier, get the sleep you need, but work to be an early riser. (I'm preaching to myself, too!)

Work. The results of a recent survey show that the average American worker is productive for only three hours in an eight-hour workday.[88] The writer actually suggests shortening the workday, but I would say shorten the time-wasters. I believe there is a place for breaks, social interaction, and other activities, but we could accomplish a lot more in an average day (which is normally more than eight hours for a pastor) if we actually worked!

Jowett gives the warning, "We may come to assume that we are really working when we are only loafing through our days."[89] We need to limit those things that distract us from our God-given tasks. It is a matter of God's glory!

Schedule your day in blocks of time. There is something intimidating or nearly impossible about trying to work a straight eight-hours at a time; but if you break it down into individual tasks, time can go by quickly and you can accomplish much more. Some suggest breaking your day into two- or four-hour blocks. I resonate with Nelson Searcy, who suggests that we work in sixty- to ninety-minute blocks of time.[90] We are much more capable of intense concentration for an hour or so at a time than for much longer periods. Work for an hour or so, then get up, walk around, use the restroom, check emails for a few minutes, and then get back to the next task.

Schedule appointments with time in mind. Normal weekly or monthly meetings can be scheduled around; it is the impromptu or one-time appointments that can cause time to slip away. Make sure you consider the time of your meetings in relation to the rest

---

[88]Melanie Curtain, "In an 8-Hour Day the Average Worker is Productive for this Many Hours," July 21, 2016, accessed January 6, 2017, http://www.inc.com/melanie-curtin/in-an-8-hour-day-the-average-worker-is-productive-for-this-many-hours.html.

[89]Jowett, *The Preacher*, 115.

[90]Searcy, *The Renegade Pastor*, 95.

of a particular day's tasks. Just the other day, I had three meetings between 8 a.m. and noon with three different students—one at 8:00, one at 10:30, and the final one at noon. The way I scheduled the meetings, there was not enough time between each one to really get anything done outside of answering menial emails. If possible, you would want to put meetings back to back, or space them out enough where there is sufficient time in between to get actual work done. Understand me, the time with students was in no way a waste, but the way I set up the meetings caused me to waste an hour or two that could have been more productive.

Make good use of mealtimes. If someone wants to meet with you or you need to spend some time with an individual, meet them for breakfast or lunch. (You ought to eat with your family in the evenings.) You need to stop and eat a meal, but it is a waste to do it alone.

Multitask. We all like to think that we are great at multitasking. Normally, we are great at doing a lot of things but none of them very well. I would normally urge you to concentrate on one task at a time until it is finished or at a good break point. However, there are some instances where multitasking is of significant value.

Waiting rooms: We all have to get our oil changed, get check-ups, etc. We often find ourselves in a waiting room of some sort. Keep a book or easily accessible work with you that allows you to put in twenty minutes of valuable time.

Commute: You probably should not read while driving between appointments, but you can listen to books, sermons, and other edifying programs. You can even cut the radio off and spend that time in prayer. Keep your eyes open; there are enough bad drivers on the road already.

If you are going somewhere that it is appropriate, take someone with you. Much mentoring and fellowship can be done on a car ride. Taking a flight somewhere? You can read entire books while flying. Be open to sharing the Gospel with those seated around you, but do not just settle for a nap unless that is what you really need.

Maintain Sabbath principles. Seriously, sometimes the most spiritual thing you can do is take a nap. You certainly need to honor the biblical principle of a Sabbath. You need to take a twenty-four-hour period and rest from your normal work, spend time worshiping the Lord, and spend relaxing time with your family. Sunday is not a day of rest for the minister, but you need to find that time period that most benefits you and your family. A refreshed minister is normally more effective than one on the edge of exhaustion.

Whatever you do, do your work heartily, as for the Lord rather than for men, knowing that from the Lord you will receive the reward of the inheritance. It is the Lord Christ whom you serve (Colossians 3:23–24).

The preparation of sermons and other teaching times rightly consumes a large portion of the pastor's everyday schedule. There are several other functions in which a pastor most likely should and will spend a substantial amount of time. The following pages highlight just a few of these. Certainly, there are numerous tasks that are not covered in detail.

Discipleship. I have already spent some time in exhorting a focus on intentional personal evangelism. However, the Great Commission calls us to do more than JUST evangelize. A pastor has to be about the work of making disciples and equipping the saints for the work of the ministry. The pastor should spend some time in making disciples of the entirety of the congregation, and this is done in the context of large teaching moments. But the pastor should also have relationships where he is pouring into small groups and individuals.

The process of choosing who to disciple on the smaller level requires careful selection. I contend that a pastor should, at any given time, have individuals or small groups where he is discipling new believers, developing new leaders, and delegating ministry responsibility to mature believers. The pastor has a limited number of hours, and Quinn correctly insists, "If a pastor is going to fulfill the mandate of the Great Commission, he must prayerfully meditate on choosing those whom he would devote his available time to nurture."[91]

If you are going to be an effective disciple-maker, you have to spend time with those you disciple. The ultimate goal is multiplication (much better than addition). Paul writes, "The things which you have heard from me in the presence of many witnesses, entrust these to faithful men who will be able to teach others also" (2 Timothy 2:2). The pastor ultimately should desire to produce disciples, develop leaders, and delegate ministry "for the equipping of the saints for the work of service" (Ephesians 4:12).

Effective administration by a pastor involves giving vision and leadership, not micromanaging. Pastors should always be looking for ways they can help other members of the body own ministry. When we delegate well, we can see several positive outcomes[92]:

> **It relieves the workload of leaders.** So many in the church take on way more than one person should have to handle. Increasing the number of workers and delegating well helps spread the labor.
>
> **It helps work get done properly.** We have all been there—so many things going at one time that few if any of them are done well. Spreading the workload helps improve the quality of ministry.
>
> **It expedites decision-making.** Delegating well and giving ownership of ministries helps decisions be made faster and more effectively. You need to make sure there are clear instructions and guidelines, but not every decision has to come across the pastor's desk.
>
> **It improves the skills of people.** Doing is most often a much better teacher than watching. Sometimes, even allowing new leaders to make mistakes is more helpful than preventive correction.
>
> **It increases productivity.** No matter how great a leader you are, we can get more done together than alone. For example,

---

[91]S. Lance Quinn, "Discipling," in MacArthur, *Pastoral Ministry*, 265.
[92]Gleaned from MacArthur, *Pastoral Ministry*, 244.

in evangelism, the pastor should evangelize, but so should every believer. If the pastor is the only one evangelizing, even effectively, the church does not grow as well as when a large number of the body are consistently sharing their faith.

It gives leaders opportunity to participate in a group. Some of the greatest blessings you receive as a pastor come from just being a participant together with the body in ministry. One of my favorite weekly meetings as a pastor was a men's Bible study where I was not the leader. Sure, certain questions would cause others to look to me for an answer, but overall, I was just another member of the class. You need these times, but they will not happen if you do not delegate ministry. Johnny Hunt explains that it really just comes down to believing in people, supporting people, investing in people, and challenging people to do the work.[93]

Counseling. Oftentimes, all counseling turns out to be is "crisis discipleship." I am convinced that the presence of biblical discipleship that begins at conversion and remains intentional and clear throughout the life of the believer would help avoid the vast majority of counseling required by the pastor and other ministerial staff. However, on the fallen side of eternity, you must recognize that you spend large amounts of time in counseling over the life of your ministry. Let me just give a few suggestions concerning the pastor and his counseling:

Capability. I have heard pastors say, "Well, I am just not qualified to do counseling." I would argue that if you are qualified for the office of pastor, you are qualified to do counseling. Listen to the problem, and then give solid, biblical counsel. Do not over-complicate the real purpose of counseling, which is to help men and women obey and walk with Jesus.

Time consumption. If you are not careful, there are those who would spend enormous amounts of your time in counseling. I suggest you limit the time of counseling to thirty

---

[93]Hunt, *Building Your Leadership Resume*, 20-24.

minutes or, at most, an hour. Most situations are not going to be improved upon after this amount of time. Normally, you have become aware of the initial problems and have enough information to give sound biblical advice. Instruct the counselee in this advice and schedule a follow-up to gauge progress.

Communicate the time limitations when you initially set up the appointment. I normally would have an hour between appointment times and let the individual know that there was someone meeting with me after him. Certainly, there are situations where you cannot put a time limit on the meeting (life or death situations), but most of the time, it is beneficial to you and the counselee to do so.

Wisdom in counseling women. We have already discussed guidelines in relation to the opposite sex, and these must be strongly held in counseling. Never counsel a woman alone without your wife or another person present. I would quickly move to put a woman under the counsel of another woman.

Take heed to guard against your counsel coming between the woman and her husband's counsel. Even a lost man has a place of authority greater than the counselor in matters of preference rather than obedience to God.

Do not allow detailed information concerning sexual sin to be discussed; it does not help the situation, so there is no need to get into sordid details.

Guard closely against the developing of an unhealthy attachment. Too many times, we have heard of the moral fall of a pastor beginning during a counseling session.

God has equipped the body. I cringe every time I hear a pastor proudly declare, "I let the professionals handle those things." Well, we are not professionals, but we are called by God and equipped by God to handle every spiritual issue, and every issue is a spiritual issue. Remember, you are equipped to give counsel from God's Word, but God also equips His body to handle every situation. I would not send my sheep to the "professionals," but I would recognize that there may be others in the body better suited for certain situations of counsel.

Hospital visitation. One of the greatest opportunities pastors have to minister to the flock is in times of sickness and particularly during a hospital stay. Some pastors have delegated this task to other staff and never darken the doors of a hospital. I believe this is a great mistake. Certainly, most churches grow to a place where the pastor or any one minister should not be asked to handle this task alone, but every pastor should avail himself of opportunities to minister in such situations. Some of your most fruitful ministry comes as a result of your genuine care during tough times. Here are a few simple reminders about hospital visitation.

It's an away game. Don't make yourself obnoxious by acting like it is your office or like you own the place. You are a visitor when you go to the hospital. Most hospitals make special concessions to pastors, but we have no right to be disrespectful when we are not allowed access.

Don't act like you are a medical expert. Certainly, most pastors spend enough time around hospitals that they begin to learn a lot of the language, positive and negative. But unless you have a medical degree, you should probably refrain from giving your "expert" medical advice.

Always knock and ask permission to enter. Privacy is not normally the top priority in a hospital, but pastors should always do all they can to respect it, especially with female members. I normally tried to take my wife with me when I visited a female church member, particularly after childbirth or any women's-specific health procedure.

Don't sit on the bed unless you are married to the patient. Even if they invite you to sit on the bed, do not do it. I hope you would never sit on someone's bed when making a home visit, so why would you do it in the hospital?

Compliment the doctor and the hospital if possible. This one goes back to Mom's old adage, "If you can't say something nice, then…." The last thing a patient needs to hear is horror stories or bad testimonies about the doctor or hospital that is treating them. Stories about the horrific pain associated with scheduled procedures should be avoided as well.

Listen and respond, but don't ask too many questions. Be short and sweet. Otherwise, you may find out more than you ever wanted to know. I can neither confirm nor deny that I learned this from experience.

Use wisdom regarding the length of your visit. If patients are waiting for their spouses by themselves, sit with them, but if family is there, come back or call and check in later. When visiting in the room, never wake anyone up; they need rest when recovering in the hospital. Leave your card or let the family know you stopped by.

Sit down if you can (not on the bed), take off your coat, and do not act like you are in a hurry. However, you probably should only stay ten or fifteen minutes. If there are several others in the room, the visit might be extended, but hospital patients need their rest, and they typically feel the need to entertain if someone stays in the room. Enter, visit, get an update on their condition, read a passage of Scripture, pray with the patient, and let them know you will continue to pray.

Take someone with you for training, information, and encouragement. In many cases, time for hospital visitation can include a decent commute and time away from the primary field of ministry. When appropriate, it can be a very conducive time to pour into those who may feel a call to some sort of ministry.

Handling the Everyday Schedule and Interruptions

As a pastor, you need to determine your priorities in speaking engagements, preparation time, visitation, and other areas. Make sure that where you spend the bulk of your time matches up with your spiritual strengths. I would suggest that you set a weekly schedule; it is important to at least try to establish some sort of routine. Certainly, there are going to be interruptions, but as I said previously, consistency breeds efficiency.

Below is a sample of how the typical week in the life of the pastor could play out:

Sunday	
6 a.m.	Wake up/Get ready/Spend time with Jesus
7 a.m.	Breakfast
8 a.m.	Arrive at church
9 a.m. – Noon	Pastoral duties
Noon – 2 p.m.	Lunch
2–5 p.m.	Rest/Spend time with family
5–8 p.m.	Evening activities
Monday	
6 a.m.	Wake up/Get ready/Spend time with Jesus
7 a.m.	Breakfast* (all non-weekend breakfast and lunch meals are a great time to schedule meetings and discipleship appointments)
8 a.m. – Noon	Study
Noon – 1 p.m.	Lunch
1-3 p.m.	Staff meeting (whole and/or individual)
3-5 p.m.	Weekly planning
Evening	Family
Tuesday	
6 a.m.	Wake up/Get ready/Spend time with Jesus
7 a.m.	Breakfast
8 a.m. – Noon	Study
Noon – 1 p.m.	Lunch

1-3 p.m.	Administrative duties, correspondence, planning
3-6 p.m.	Home
6-8 p.m.	Visitation appointments (evangelistic, prospects, etc.)
Wednesday	
6 a.m.	Wake up/Get ready/Spend time with Jesus
7 a.m.	Breakfast
8 a.m. – Noon	Study
Noon –1 p.m.	Lunch
1-4 p.m.	Long-range planning/Meetings
4-8 p.m.	Counseling, mid-week meetings, leadership training
Thursday	
6 a.m.	Wake up/Get ready/Spend time with Jesus
7 a.m.	Breakfast
8 a.m. – Noon	Study
Noon – 1 p.m.	Lunch
1-5 p.m.	Any remaining administrative tasks, correspondence, hospital and shut-in visitation
Evening	Family
Friday	
6 a.m.	Wake up/Get ready/Spend time with Jesus
7 a.m.	Breakfast
8 a.m. – Noon	Study
Noon	Begin Sabbath period of rest, not legalistic, but away from normal activities other than genuine emergencies. Spend time with your family, relax, and spend extra time with the Lord.

Saturday	
Morning	Continued time of rest and time with family
Afternoon	Continued family time, children's extracurricular activities, honey-do list
Evening	Final time with sermon, then relax and go to bed early

I know many of you, if not most or even all of you, are thinking that there is no way you can hold such a schedule. The above schedule comes out to more than a fifty-hour work week. I would estimate a pastor can expect on a typical week to spend about sixty hours in legitimate ministry work. It is imperative that pastors put aside as many distractions as possible, but keep room for rest, relaxation, and replenishment. The above schedule does not even mention the drop-by appointments, genuine emergencies, or deaths. Not to mention the numerous other demands on the pastor and his time. Some would just give up on any kind of schedule, but I would argue that is all the more reason to set a schedule and guard it well.

How to view interruptions. When you are trying to maintain a schedule, sometimes it is frustrating when interruptions occur. The key is to guard your schedule but understand that, in ministry, oftentimes, interruptions are the ministry. There are steps that pastors can take to limit interruptions or at least control them and deal with them at certain times of the day and/or week. There are certain things in ministry that require a complete interruption of the schedule. The members of your church cannot schedule accidents, sudden sickness, crisis situations, and certainly not death.

As much as I would exhort you to take a consistent day off, it is not an excuse to neglect a grieving family in your congregation. For example, if your normal days off are Friday afternoon and Saturday, and you have a church member die on Friday afternoon, you should not neglect that person's family but rather take opportunity to minister to them. I would contend also that you should not feel guilty if you take some time the next Monday afternoon to rest and spend time with your own family. The key rests in your ability to preserve balance between faithfully ministering to your family, your flock, and yourself.

Communicate your schedule: If you desire to guard your schedule, you must communicate it effectively to your family and church members. Most church members understand that the pastor needs ample time to study for and prepare sermons. If you communicate to the body the need to give your mornings to God in that preparation, they can help you guard it.

Enlist others in guarding your schedule: The use of an administrative assistant can be a great blessing to the pastor. The assistant can help keep and guard the schedule effectively. A pastor needs to be available for members, but an assistant can be a buffer between the phone, emails, and unexpected visitors. Other staff and church employees can help guard each other's time by recognizing the tasks and people that are consistently interrupting the plan. The sharing of such responsibilities helps limit the impact on the schedule.

Make sure you guard your schedule: If you communicate a schedule to your family and the members of your church, and enlist others to help you guard your schedule, you must be consistent in guarding it yourself. If others see you not taking your schedule seriously, they will feel no need to help guard it either.

Bisagno reminds the pastor, "People are never an interruption of our ministry—they are our ministry." However, he adds, "It is your responsibility to determine what is and what is not an emergency."[94] You, as the pastor, have to discern whether a situation merits changing your schedule.

---

[94]Bisagno, *Pastor's Handbook*, 70, 72.

Conclusion

There are so many other aspects of pastoral ministry that could be discussed, but understanding the reality of the assignment is key. The reality being that no pastor has ever served or even existed who could handle the demands of ministry in his own strength. The tasks are unending and nearly immeasurable. The scrutiny on every action is nearly unbearable at times. The pain and disappointment can often be overwhelming. Pastoral ministry is a task only accomplished by the man who walks filled with and empowered by the Holy Spirit.

These and many other difficulties require the pastor who desires to do everyday ministry to walk daily with Jesus in a real and intimate way. He must be firm in his conviction that God has called and invited Him to the task. The pastor must display and maintain integrity in all of his everyday actions. He must make sure every decision accomplishes the primary tasks that God has placed upon him.

As you walk in everyday ministry, make sure you walk with Jesus, take care of your family, feed the flock, care for the sheep, and utilize every moment as unto the Lord. Minister in such a way that, when this brief life is over, you might cry out as the apostle Paul:

> *I have fought the good fight, I have finished the course, I have kept the faith; in the future there is laid up for me the crown of righteousness, which the Lord, the righteous Judge, will award to me on that day; and not only to me, but also to all who have loved His appearing (2 Timothy 4:7-8).*

Bibliography

A Pastor's Guide to Text-Driven Preaching. Fort Worth, TX: Seminary Hill Press, 2016.

Adams, Jay. "Editorial: Good Preaching is Hard Work." *The Journal of Pastoral Practice* 4, no. 2, 1980.

Allen, Jason. *Discerning Your Call To Ministry: How to Know for Sure and What to Do About It*. Chicago, IL: Moody, 2016.

Baxter, Richard. *The Reformed Pastor*, Revised and Abridged by William Brown. Glasgow: William Collins, 1829.

Bisagno, John. *The Pastor's Handbook*. Nashville, TN: Broadman & Holman, 2011.

Bounds, E.M. *Power through Prayer* rev. ed. Grand Rapids, MI: Zondervan, 1962.

Bridges, Charles. *The Christian Ministry*. London: Seeley, Burnside, and Seeley, 1844.

Bryant, James and Mac Brunson. *The New Guidebook for Pastors*. Nashville, TN: Broadman & Holman, 2007.

Cowen, Gerald P. *Who Rules the Church?* Nashville, TN: Broadman & Holman, 2003.

Criswell, W.A. *Criswell's Guidebook for Pastors.* Nashville, TN: Broadman Press, 1980.

Curtain, Melanie. "In an 8-Hour Day the Average Worker is Productive for this Many Hours," July 21, 2016, accessed January 6, 2017, http://www.inc. com/melanie-curtin/in-an-8-hour-day-the-average-worker-is-productive-for-this-many-hours.html.

Draper, Jimmy. *Don't Quit Before You Finish.* Franklin, TN: Clovercroft, 2015.

Howard, Jaqueline. "Americans devote more than 10 hours a day to screen time, and growing," June 30, 2016, accessed January 5, 2017, http://www. cnn.com/2016/06/30/health/americans-screen-time-nielsen/.

Hunt, Johnny. *Building Your Leadership Resume: Developing the Legacy That Will Outlast You.* Nashville, TN: Broadman & Holman, 2009.

Iorg, Jeff. *Is God Calling Me.* Nashville, TN: Broadman & Holman, 2008.

Jowett, J.H. *The Preacher His Life and Work.* New York: Harper & Brothers, 1912.

Kiker, Tommy. "'Yeah, I'll Pray For You Later' – How To Avoid The Lie," *Theological Matters* (February 16, 2016). Accessed March 10, 2017. http://theologicalm-atters.com/2016/02/16/yeah-ill-pray-for-you-later-how-to-avoid-the-lie/.

Lutzer, Edwin. *Pastor to Pastor.* Grand Rapids, MI: Kregel, 2008.

MacArthur, John and the Master's Seminary Faculty. *Pastoral Ministry: How to Shepherd Biblically.* Nashville, TN: Thomas Nelson, 2005.

MacArthur, John. *The Master's Plan for the Church.* Chicago: Moody, 2008.

_____. "The Qualifications for a Pastor, Part 2; Noble Character, Part 2," on December 13, 1992, accessed February 4, 2017, https://www.gty.org/library/sermons-library/56-8/the-qualifications-for-a-pastor-part-2-noble-character-part-2.

Oates, Wayne. *The Christian Pastor.* Philadelphia, PA: Westminster Press, 1951.

Owen, John. *Sin & Temptation.* Portland, OR: Multnomah, 1983.

Patterson, Paige. *A Field Guide for a Dangerous Call.* Fort Worth, TX: Seminary Hill Press, 2014.

Patterson, Paige. *Living in Hope of Eternal Life: An Exposition of the Book of Titus.* Eugene, OR: Wipf & Stock, 1968.

Patterson, Paige. *So You Have Been Called to a Church.* Wake Forest, NC: Magnolia Hill Papers, 1996.

Patterson, Paige, Thomas White, and L.R. Scarborough. *Calling Out the Called.* Fort Worth, TX: Seminary Hill Press, 2008.

Queen, Matt. *Everyday Evangelism.* Fort Worth, TX: Seminary Hill Press, 2015.

Sanders, J. Oswald. *Spiritual Leadership: Principles of Excellence for Every Believer.* Chicago, IL: Moody, 2007.

Scarborough, L.R. *Recruits for World Conquest.* New York: Fleming H. Revell, 1914.

Searcy, Nelson. *The Renegade Pastor: Abandoning Average in Your Life and Ministry.* Grand Rapids, MI: Baker, 2013.

Spurgeon, C.H. *Lectures to My Students,* Reprint. Grand Rapids, MI: Zondervan, 1972.

_____. "Serving the Lord with Gladness," in *Metropolitan Tabernacle Pulpit*. London: Passmore and Alabaster, 1868; reprint, Pasadena, TX: Pilgrim Publications, 1989.

Stott, John. *The Preacher's Portrait: Some New Testament Word Studies*. Grand Rapids, MI: Eerdmans, 1988.

_____. "Ideals of Pastoral Ministry." Roy Zuck, *Vital Ministry Issues: Examining Concerns and Conflicts in Ministry*. Eugene, OR: Wipf & Stock, 2004.

Tozer, A.W. *Tozer for the Christian Leader: A 365-Day Devotional*, compiled by Ron Eggert. Chicago, IL: Moody, 2015.

Tucker, Austin B. *A Primer for Pastors: A Handbook for Strengthening Ministry Skills*. Grand Rapids, MI: Kregel, 2004.

Wilder, Terry. "What a Minister of the Gospel Must Be." *Answering the Call: Examining God's Call to Christian Service*. Kansas City, MO: Midwestern Baptist Theological Seminary, 2010.

Yarnell, Malcolm and Karen Yarnell. "Spiritual Formation through Family Worship: The Heart of the Matter." In *Everyday Parenting*, edited by Alex Sibley, 53-66. Fort Worth, TX: Seminary Hill Press, 2017.

Other resources by Seminary Hill Press...

Preaching Tools
by David L. Allen
An annotated survey of commentaries and preaching resources for every book of the Bible.

A Pastor's Guide to Text-Driven Preaching
by Southwestern's School of Preaching Faculty
The what, how, and why of effective text-driven preaching.

Everyday Evangelism
by Matt Queen
Encouragement, insight, and practical steps for creating a culture of everyday evangelism in your church.

A Field Guide for a Dangerous Call
by Paige Patterson
Biblical principles for avoiding the pitfalls of ministry.

For more information on these and other titles, visit SeminaryHillPress.com.